FOREWARD BY EVA█████ ████ █████
CO-FOUNDER (AWAKENING HOPE MINISTRIES)

DEATH *of a* YELLOW PAGE SALESMAN

FROM LOST TO FOUND-
FILLED TO OVERFLOWING

Patti,

"May your life always be
"Filled to Overflowing!"

Paul Lindstrom

FOREWARD BY EVANGELIST DEAN GOOSSEN
CO-FOUNDER (AWAKENING HOPE MINISTRIES)

DEATH of a YELLOW PAGE SALESMAN

FROM LOST TO FOUND—
FILLED TO OVERFLOWING

BEST-SELLING AUTHOR
PAUL T. NEUSTROM

Published by Best Seller Publishing®, St. Augustine, FL
Best Seller Publishing® is a registered trademark.
Printed in the United States of America.
ISBN: 978-1-959840-03-9

For more information, please write:
Best Seller Publishing®
53 Marine Street
St. Augustine, FL 32084
or call 1 (626) 765-9750
Visit us online at: www.BestSellerPublishing.org

TABLE OF CONTENTS

FOREWORD

PACKED FULL OF insightful gold nuggets, this book will remind you of the valuable difference between theory and experience. With a perfect combination of inspiration, strategy, wisdom, faith, and a call to action, Paul Neustrom eloquently weaves together a work of art that can ensure your business or ministry will never be the same.

There are some seasons in life that just "are what they are." However, I am reminded of the account in Exodus when the Israelites who had left Egypt were preparing to enter the Promised Land, and their season in the desert was turning out to be much longer than what they'd originally intended, even to the point where almost an entire generation missed out on what was promised to them. This is the kind of book that will ensure that fear and lack of knowledge won't cause that to happen to you!

The Bible promises that God has a plan for our lives. Some take that to mean we must do nothing and wait for everything to happen on its own. Sometimes we forget that we have a part to play in making the most of each season of life (even the hard seasons). If God tells you to wait, then wait. However, more often than not, we are guilty of not being aggressive and taking the bull by the horns. We should make it our life's goal to not leave any potential on the table when we die. When we seek the Lord and ask Him to reveal things to us, we often find that He rewards us with ideas and strategies that we may not have come up with on our own.

This book will help equip you to trust in the Lord and fulfill *everything* He has called you to do. It will sharpen your faith and build your character. The pages are dripping with experience, wisdom, and humility. I believe the Holy Spirit will speak to you as you read this book, and even remind you of things you read at opportune times.

I encourage you, as you read and follow Paul along this journey, to grab a pen and paper and write down what is stirred up in you. You may find yourself receiving a pep talk from Paul that is making you accountable to your potential and breaking you free from the chains that have anchored you to your failures. You might actually give yourself permission to step out and chase your dreams and, most of all, be reminded of what fulfillment really looks like so you don't achieve your goals and still feel empty.

This journey lays a solid foundation that hope and purpose are found in Christ alone. May everything we do bring Him glory!

—Evangelist Dean Goossen
Co-founder of Awakening Hope Ministries

INTRODUCTION: CATCH THE WAVE

I WAS INSPIRED to write this book when I moved to California for a short time. There, the culture of outdoor sports, which includes surfing, is alive and exciting. I love how they call one of the coolest surfing maneuvers "Hang Ten." It requires surfers to position their feet on the surfboard in a unique way. The back of the board is covered by a massive wave, which allows the rider to walk to the front of the board, "Hanging Ten" toes over the front edge of the surfboard. This maneuver is the embodiment of this book on marketing, in which you go from lost to found and empty to full, not just in business but also in life.

Just as with surfing, your business can catch the wave of success and continue going, allowing prosperity to flow. "Hanging Ten" and "Killing It" are the same, just different ways of expressing it. Can you see the vivid mental picture that translates into what you, as a business owner, desire to achieve? Now is the time to take action and "Catch the Wave."

Imagine life filled to overflowing; how do you go from empty to fulfilled? *Photo credit: pixabay.com/images/id-1477175/*

WHERE I CAME FROM

Marketing, advertising, consulting, and training have been my main occupations. For the past forty years, I have advised and consulted with more than 10,000 business owners. Having grown up in the Midwest, I attended the University of Nebraska-Lincoln on a gymnastics scholarship and then went to the University of Kansas in Lawrence.

My main focus for most of my career has been with "yellow pages" (phone directories), which proved to be largely successful. Unfortunately, I soon found the industry swallowed up with the rise of Google. The greatest advantage I offer is my ability to transfer the skills and knowledge I acquired in the physical directories to an understanding of how to dominate with online directories and media.

The ability to connect with our clients and customers in a personal way—the human side of business—is incredibly important. I feel it needs to be done in an intimate way, and learning this skill changed my life and my career. Working with this focus over the years has allowed me to become a top producer in many different companies.

WHO I AM NOW

I am a speaker, podcaster, business consultant, and marketing advisor with more than forty years of experience in marketing and sales. My mission is to help 10,000 marketing coaches start and grow their own businesses so that they can have a massive impact on their clients and give back to their passions.

My recent major achievement has been my work writing several books and courses. I focused my efforts on several key areas while I was teaching entrepreneurs and business owners ways to grow their businesses. Through this book, you will learn how to grow and transform yourself by gaining inspiration from the small, still voice of God and taking action according to it.

My desire is to help people learn how to transform their lives by tapping into the creative energies of God. Learning the principles of marketing, developing a core passion for your life, and then acting on it to bring zest to living. Promoting what I believe in has been my life's mission since I was twenty-one. As you will see, my life has been mainly about achieving this goal.

WHO THIS IS FOR

With the constantly changing sales industry, people who are interested in sales and digital marketing need to be willing to adapt to change and develop a few fundamental skills. This book offers you a guide on how to do just that, especially for those who are having a hard time changing.

A lot of times, marketers and business owners find themselves sifting through hours of content, only to receive technical advice. These sources profess knowledge, but they often lack practical experience. Ultimately, I achieved my success through developing my practical experience in contrast to building book knowledge.

With this concept in mind, this book is devoted to helping you empty yourself out so that you can be filled. Enjoy the entertainment of reading my stories, which I gained from working with hundreds of media sales reps and thousands of business owners. Take some time to reflect on these principles, and they will truly change your perception of your path in business and, more importantly, in your personal life.

NAVIGATING THE PRINCIPLES OF MY BOOK

Among the vast array of self-help books that promote their own methods of being successful, very few speak of an understanding of effective communication and why these principles work. These principles work systematically, and you will be able to apply these secrets to every aspect of your life. It is transformational when we understand the way we communicate with others, which is often governed by how we talk to ourselves. These principles work in all aspects of your life, even marketing and business. Marketing is my specialty, and I am writing this book to show how the power of words will change your life.

Beginning with the inspiration for the title of this book, I will transition to the story of a significant change that happened in my life. Along with this, I describe the impact of a unique circumstance involving a loved one where recovering from a significant loss took a major toll on my life. Going from lost to found is something I not only helped business owners do, but I learned how to do it in my life. Finding your passion and purpose as a business owner or entrepreneur is one of the most meaningful goals you can achieve.

Next, we will cover how to create momentum in your business, discussing marketing principles that will allow you to create your own unique business strategy. Rather than taking a formulaic approach, this section provides guidelines and puts customers' perspectives at the forefront.

Finally, we will discuss a central issue that held me back, along with an infinite number of other people. That issue is *fear*, an emotion that can sometimes protect you but, at the same time, tremendously limit your abilities. Ultimately, fear is often a response to change, which can be either a setback or a blessing depending on how you deal with it.

Your response to change will impact you in so many dynamic ways. As someone working in business, you will find that your industry constantly shifts as demand changes. I know that my industry did, as I suddenly had to make the change from working in traditional media to entering the widely changing digital world. I believe that this book will teach you the proper response to change—embracing it instead of avoiding it.

Ultimately, my main goal is to empower you as an individual. Rather than giving you clear-cut formulas and shortcuts, I want to help you discover the lessons I have learned through personal experience. This is so you can understand the fundamentals in order to avoid potential pitfalls and start to triumph in life. As Dave Ramsey says in several of his books, he needs to teach you the spiritual principles first before he can teach you how to manage your money. Once you know these concepts, you can build your own unique, successful strategy and strengthen your overall abilities in marketing and self-leadership.

As an entrepreneur and businessperson, you most likely already have certain strengths and an understanding of your field. The potential to become widely successful is already in you. Through this book, I believe you will be able to strengthen these skills and develop more momentum in both your work and your personal life, to the point of overflowing.

PREFACE

WORLD EVENTS AND developing technology have changed the way we interact with our friends, our families, and our loved ones. As online interactions have entered and begun to dominate, life as we know it has changed. What were once choices have now become requirements. People say we live in an online world that's more connected than ever before, but are we, personally? The sad truth is that we are also more isolated than ever before in recorded history.

Struggling as a victim is not an empowering position but one that leaves you with self-pity and holds you back. With this focus comes the problems and the frustrations, where we feel that the world is against us. This is a tough place to be, although we have all experienced loss to some extent in our lives. This book is how I came to deal with it.

When wealth is lost, nothing is lost;
when health is lost, something is lost;
when character is lost, all is lost.
—Billy Graham

INSPIRATION FOR THIS BOOK

CERTAIN ENDEAVORS BECOME defining moments in our lives. One of mine, the trip that has meant the most to me, was my trek to the Holy Land. At the time I traveled there, my career in the yellow pages had pretty well ended, and I felt really empty. Personally, viewing the sites of significant historical events was unlike any vacation I had ever taken.

Traveling with a group of seventy Christians, I went to more than sixty places, including the Church of the Nativity and the Sea of Galilee. However, the one that stood out to me above all the others was Jacob's Well. Many people have visited this site because of its well-known story in the Bible when a Samaritan woman named Photini had one of the most dramatic meetings with a man who should not have been talking to her. The story of the woman at the well contains the longest written account of a conversation with Jesus Christ. She was a woman whose life was entangled in securing earthly pleasures. Having gone through five husbands and now with a sixth man who wasn't her husband, she was never fulfilled by what she had. This reminded me of my own life, as I was always looking for more but was never able to satisfy my tremendous thirst. But with her, all it took was one encounter, a meaningful conversation with "Jesus the Christ" to transform her life.

When you walk into the Church of St. Photini, which is located inside a monastery, you see a beautiful, ornate temple. Amid all the beauty of the surroundings, the marble and all the icons are beyond description.

Located directly beneath the altar is the actual well where Jesus and Photini had their long conversation together. What's impressive is that it is a very rustic setting—something like you would expect to see from the very beginnings of Christian antiquity. The life-changing words spoken by Jesus Christ are recorded in John 4:13–15 (KJV): *Jesus answered and said unto her, "Whosoever drinketh of this water shall thirst again, but whosoever drinketh of the water that I shall give him shall never thirst; but the water that I shall give him shall be in him a well of water springing up into everlasting life." The woman said unto Him, "Sir, give me this water, that I thirst not, neither come hither to draw."*[1]

The story about the woman at the well continues, but the result of it is revealing because it says: *The woman left her water pot because of all the things He said to her and she went her way back to the city, and said to everyone: "Come, see a man who told me everything I ever did. Could this be the Christ?"*—John 4:29 (NKJV)[2]

Jacob's Well

[1] https://www.kingjamesbibleonline.org/John-4-13_4-15/
[2] https://biblehub.com/nkjv/john/4.htm

The Greek Orthodox St. Photini Church at Bir Ya'qub

Church of St. Photini in Palestine

The church above is where Jacob's Well is located in Palestine. After recalling this story, I tasted the water, which seemed sweet. After spending some time taking all this in, I climbed the stairs to go back up to the church. Then I saw a large icon of Christ and his mother, Mary, at the top of the stairs. Jesus was sitting in a fountain, where water was pouring out of him. It was at this moment that a promise from God came to me: "Your life will be filled to overflowing!"

Let me describe the impact these words have had on my life since then, because God had a lot to show me before He fulfilled this promise. Along with the impact of these words, the encounter at the well had a dynamic effect on Photini, the woman at the well. She became an absolute fool for Christ.

She knew firsthand and believed that this man was The Christ, the Messiah, the Son of the living God, and she declared this to everyone she came into contact with. Many disciples recognized her as a woman equal to the Apostles. She went on to win her entire family over to Christ and eventually became martyred because nothing could shut her up. This realization helped me find what I was looking for, the hope and fulfillment I was looking for in my life.

When I was growing up, I faced negative situations, and my mother would say, "Look for something good to come out of it!" At first, I found those words to be unsettling, but when applied, the silver lining usually showed through. Because of those words and the way my life was changed by a miraculous transformation, I was motivated to write this book.

This alone will not magically change your perspective, but it can be an encouragement for you to start pressing forward. I have faced dire circumstances in my life, including losing my job, my house, my car, and my wife—all at the same time. I just wanted to quit. However, I decided to keep going. Something deep inside me was encouraging me to go on. What changed my vision of myself so I could overcome my fears and my past? That is what this book is about.

Through hard work and a decision to not be paralyzed by fear, you can overcome the situation you are in and not see yourself as a victim. As I show in my stories, taking control of your life as a victor instead of a victim is a gradual process, and it won't always be perfect. Combined with the tips I am about to provide you, taking these steps will start you on a journey that will begin to transform you. Now let me tell you the rest of my story.

PART I

DEATH OF A YELLOW PAGE SALESMAN

THE PLAY *DEATH of a Salesman* addresses the loss of a man's identity and his inability to embrace change in the world and himself.[3]

    This popular tragedy from the 1940s puts a spotlight on Willy Loman, who works as a traveling salesman. From the start, he is disappointed with his life and appears to have backslid from his prime. As he pursues the American Dream for himself and his children, he finds that he falls short, and ultimately he takes drastic measures and ends his own life.

---

[3]   Miller, Arthur. *Death of a Salesman*, 1949.

WHO IS WILLY LOMAN?

The main character, Willy, is like most salespeople, motivated to become great through many accomplishments and for recognition. This is the fuel that lights the fire of desire within them because they place appearance and the end result over a quality life and enjoying the work they do.

An athlete or person of renown past the prime of life can be hard to watch. This is because winning, success, and fame are the ideals of American culture. In response, we fear pity and our own mortality. We often dream of a successful career and a life with abundance and wealth. Don't we desire this so we can have the freedom to do whatever we want, whenever we want? Along with this, we want these attractive attributes so we will become popular and well liked. When we don't have these trappings of success, we feel that we are missing something.

In reviewing the play *Death of a Salesman*, one critic noted, "Society tries to teach that, if people are rich and well liked, they will be happy. Because of this, Willy thought that money would make him happy. He never bothered to try to be happy with what he had."

I have been in a similar place in life where I lost all order and was seeking normalcy again. In a nutshell,

I was over sixty and financially unstable. More importantly, I was unable to get past my self-importance and reliance on memories from the past. As one reviewer wrote of Willy Loman in the play, "The more he indulges in the illusion, the harder it is for him to face reality."

PUBLISHING LIGHT GOES ON

Let me reflect back on my career working in the yellow pages. I have experienced an incredible journey that eventually allowed me to use my gifts to help develop other owners' businesses, as well as the Kingdom of God.

My career began when I helped start a business in college known as University Photography, where we would take pictures at fraternity and sorority parties. Back in the '70s, it was a very successful party-picture business. We had one of the highest average order rates for party pictures in the country—5.5 pictures per person.

Because of this, we were always busy on the weekends. Every Saturday at midnight, we rushed by flying our film from Lawrence, Kansas, to the Kansas City International Airport so it could be flown to Oklahoma City to be developed. Then we rushed back at 6 a.m. to pick up our order from the return flight. Afterward, we would deliver the proof sheets with donuts and coffee to the sleepy-eyed partiers who were at the event the night before.

University Photography was a phenomenal business model, but we noticed a genuine need in the market. The only pictorial publication of students was in the yearbook, which would only come out at the end of the year. It was not easy to find the new students in it and it was always at least half a year late.

In response, we created a photo yearbook known as the *Greek Directory*. We took the photographs of the pledges in front of their Greek houses two weeks after they pledged. It was great because we put each of the names of the freshman pledges from the front to the back row, left to right. That way, Terry (for example) could call Susie at the Pi Phi house and say, "Hey Susie, this is Terry and I'm an ATO and I am on page 7 in the front row and the far right … will you go out with me?" It was a great introduction and way before online dating started. Our advertising publication took off, right from the start.

My responsibility was to sell advertising space in the *Greek Directory* since I studied marketing and advertising at the University of Kansas. Three other people worked with me, and I trained them all how to sell. Because I was outselling everybody several times over, the owner made me the sales manager. I remember my third sales presentation vividly. It was with a high-end jeweler on Massachusetts Street in Lawrence.

In this presentation, I pointed out that there were more than 2,500 Greeks and that the jeweler was making a huge decision about whether he wanted to be in front of this year's pledge class. They were the most affluent group and had the highest disposable income, so I posed the question, "Are they *not* the best prospects for your jewelry business?"

Emphatically, I pointed out that he was making a decision that I was convinced would have a dramatic impact on his company—not only for the duration of their freshman year but over the next three and a half years through their sophomore, junior, and senior years, and maybe beyond.

The revealing of this principle to me and many others is why I have been in publishing ever since. In college, what I was doing was an early form of directory advertising. Little did I know that the yellow pages industry would explode in the next five years, which was right after the AT&T telephone conglomerate was broken up in 1984. It was divided into "Baby Bells" to break the power of the monopoly of telephone directories. This is what caused the yellow pages and telephone directories to come on so strongly and accelerate rapidly.

Providentially, it was in 1987 that I jumped into this business opportunity with both feet because I had just come off the Christian mission field as a missionary and was ready to make some serious money. Boy, did I ever. I worked with yellow pages for almost thirty years and was a top 1% earner. It was going great until the bottom dropped out of my life.

HITTING ROCK BOTTOM

The story of the lowest point of my career I will remember forever. While sitting at my desk in my home office, I was thinking about how I had retired from the yellow pages and how God had always taken care of me. I remember thinking that I had a roof over my head, great health, and friends and family who loved me. Throughout the past, things had always turned out for me. However, this time I was very concerned for my life because while I could see I wasn't living on the streets yet, I knew that it could become a very real possibility.

Just ten minutes before, I was carrying things out to my car to go somewhere, and I forgot something. When I went back to the car, I found I had lost my wallet with my ID, all of my credit cards, and all the money

I had—except for $15 that I had in my desk upstairs. My bank account contained only $100, and the bank was a half-hour drive away. Besides this, my car was overheating every time I drove it, and I had already spent practically all my money to fix it. Since my job was doing outside sales, I couldn't work without a car.

How did I get myself into this position? After a 29-year love-hate relationship selling yellow page ads in the back of the phone books, it had all come to an end. Google had slowly and effectively killed my work.

I had hung in for an extra two years, peddling yellow page ads in remote sections of North Idaho. You know the pristine places with no cellular service or very little coverage? The only way I could get business owners to talk to me was by helping them with their online marketing for *free*! This included how to get listed and have a strong presence on the largest and most dominant search engine in the world, Google.

THE DECLINE OF THE YELLOW PAGE PHONE DIRECTORIES

Some may be asking, "When did you see the decline of the yellow pages?" It was at the very beginning, looking back. Computers were all the rage in the mid-'80s. I had completed computer school several years before, and I saw that computers were a force to be reckoned with. I gained a keen interest in them. In fact, I had a fascination with computers initially because of some Bible software I was using.

I had a database of the Holy Bible on a 5¼-inch floppy disk, and you could look up any verse with this program. For example, if you typed in "John 3:16," it would go right to that verse. The guy who showed me this program showed me that verse. Then he typed, "For God so loved." It showed every place in the Bible where that phrase appeared. My mind was blown by how computers had the power to sort through this data.

This led me to enroll in school, where I learned how to use the most popular software like dBase III+ (database program), Peach Tree (accounting program), and WordPerfect (word processing program). I ended up graduating with the highest GPA in the school. For some reason, I had a real knack for computers, but I never had a desire to write code. I thought I could go out and sell my wares and serve ten times more clients and scale my business. I was working with 1,500 clients when I ended up selling franchises several years later.

This was at the beginning of online media, and we started seeing online directories like Google, Yahoo, and Bing. Little did I know at that time how much computers would play in the revolution of a culture now totally filled with technology.

The global pandemic has succeeded in pointing out that we are indeed in the middle of a technological revolution.
—*Forbes*[4]

THE FOUNDATION OF GOOGLE

The platform on which Google is now the world's largest monopoly was totally dependent on phone directories for its starting point. Back in the mid-1990s and early 2000s, all the data from the print directories were added to Google to provide it with relevant content. As a business owner, you had to have a business license and a business phone line to even speak with a phone book representative, or you were not otherwise a verifiable business. If you didn't have these items, you could not be in the white or yellow pages and were not considered legitimate.

Before cell phone use, no one published private phone lines for businesses. The phone companies had

---

[4] https://www.forbes.com/sites/forbesbusinessdevelopmentcouncil/2020/10/14/recognizing-the-technological-revolution-and-preparing-for-the-next-economy/?sh=39608f0c3965

the business owners trained to do it their way or hit the highway. As a yellow pages salesman, I saw people only once a year and they had to decide right away or they were left out of the book. People who are seniors now remember paying upward of 25 cents per minute for long-distance calls. As cell phones appeared in the late '80s and early '90s, things changed.

I really miss the days when business owners would pick up their phones because there was no caller ID. There wasn't any voicemail, and we didn't even have fax machines. Things were simpler. We seemed to have more time to invest in human interactions, compared to now.

However, the decline of yellow pages became really serious around 2009, when the recession hit. When people started to search the internet on their smartphones, that is when things really started to change in a big way.

SMARTPHONES ULTIMATELY DESTROYED TRADITIONAL PUBLISHING

How did the smartphone—the iPhone and Android phones—ultimately destroy traditional publishing? Why is it taking over all personal computing? Has business changed dramatically from the influence of cell phones? Look at the average amount of screen time we spend in the U.S. on our electronic devices. The main factors that account for the smartphones' dominance are mobility and power; also ease of use, convenience, and productivity are all reasons cited for its rise to power.

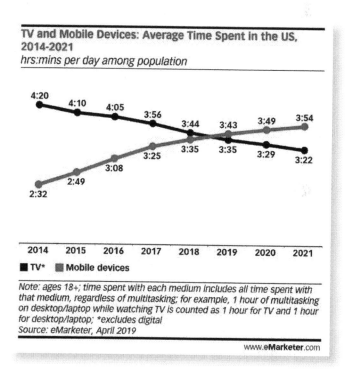

TV and Mobile Devices: Average Time Spent in the US, 2014-2021
hrs:mins per day among population

TV*: 4:20 (2014), 4:10 (2015), 4:05 (2016), 3:56 (2017), 3:44 (2018), 3:43 (2019), 3:49 (2020), 3:54 (2021)

Mobile devices: 2:32 (2014), 2:49 (2015), 3:08 (2016), 3:25 (2017), 3:35 (2018), 3:35 (2019), 3:29 (2020), 3:22 (2021)

■ TV*   ■ Mobile devices

*Note: ages 18+; time spent with each medium includes all time spent with that medium, regardless of multitasking; for example, 1 hour of multitasking on desktop/laptop while watching TV is counted as 1 hour for TV and 1 hour for desktop/laptop; *excludes digital*
Source: eMarketer, April 2019

www.**eMarketer**.com

The fact that you had the capability to take a phone anywhere you went back in the mid-'80s became an incredible tool for business. It was also a great convenience, allowing you to stay in touch with family and friends, and for the security it provided to mothers who wanted to stay in close communication with their children. It revolutionized not only the way we do business but also the way we do life.

The effect it has had in empowering mobility is also controversial. You are now instantly able to get in touch with people at any moment of the day and, sadly, night. Husbands and men who had cell phones joked about having to carry an electronic restraint. We won't even go into the destruction this device has had on marriages and how it facilitates infidelity. However, cell phones don't destroy relationships, people do.

The mobile phone has enabled us to do everything on one device, with a million times more power than what the computers of yesterday had. We each depend on our "device" because it is not just a phone but also your camera, rolodex, and personal secretary. It's more than your travel agent because it can even give you directions in a foreign country. Instead of waiting a week for snail mail to go through the post office, now we can scan a document and send it in seconds. The most powerful aspect of the device is the promise of the freedom it heralds. What people want to ignore is the sheer power and control our devices have exerted over us through our dependence upon them.

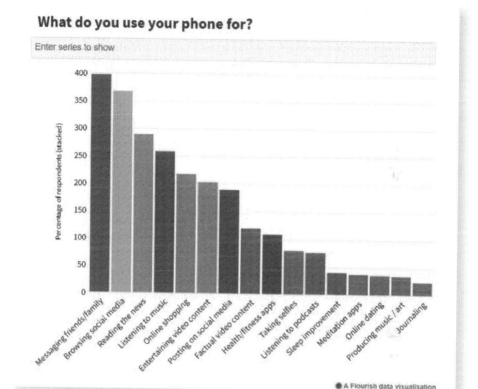

Data from September 24, 2021, indicates that the number of mobile devices is expected to reach 18.22 billion by 2025, an increase of 4.2 billion devices over 2020 levels.—Statista.com

Photo credit: A Flourish Data

The reason for the dependence is that handheld cellular phones process at a faster rate than a lot of laptops or PCs. Someone will soon be writing a book called *The Death of a PC Salesperson.*

The website Zme Science published an article called "Your mobile phone is millions of times more powerful than the Apollo 11 guidance computers."[5] The article stated, "You wouldn't be wrong in saying an iPhone could be used to guide 120,000,000 Apollo-era spacecraft to the moon, all at the same time."

However, when it begins to erode our personal freedoms, then you understand what it means to be a slave of technology. Working with a cell phone every day, all day, made me feel like a bondservant to this device. Taking a break from it on the weekends felt like a vacation. The freedom we gain simply by curbing the use of our devices is amazing. Now, as you know, it can dramatically affect how the world monitors us, interacts with us, and controls us.

pic by stphnwlkr.co

"It's amazing to think we went to the moon in 1969."
Photo credit: stphnwlkr.com

---

5   https://www.zmescience.com/science/news-science/smartphone-power-compared-to-apollo-432

KILLING IT ONLINE

Technology can be a double-edged sword. It can be a help or a hindrance in your life, depending on how you use it or how you balance it in your life. Several times in this book I will mention my website KillingItOnline.com.

What does "Killing It Online" really mean? It actually has a double connotation: you can do incredibly well and be successful doing business online, but you can also go too far. When your passion for technology begins to destroy the very things that were meant to be freedoms, it gets everything backward. When you begin to prioritize work over your personal life and health, which in turn pressures you to move at a faster, unhealthy pace, this creates a vicious cycle. When your priorities are in proper alignment, you will be more successful with your business online, while taking care of yourself and those close to you.

WHY ARE CEOS UNPLUGGING?

CEOs are unplugging from online interactions in a world that has become too wired. Why do highly successful people, specifically CEOs, who shun technology succeed by doing this?

Warren Buffet, one of the wealthiest people in the world and CEO of Berkshire Hathaway, doesn't like owning a smartphone (according to *USA Today*[6]). Mikhail Prokhorov, billionaire and former owner of the New York Nets (now known as the NBA Brooklyn Nets), does not use a cell phone. He also prefers handwritten letters over emails, the *New York Post* reported in an interview. On the TV show *60 Minutes*, Prokhorov said, "I don't use a computer. We have too much information, and it's really impossible to filter it."[7]

Dan Henry, a self-made multimillionaire, revealed in his best-selling book *Digital Millionaire Secrets* how he built an eight-figure business selling his knowledge online. However, Dan found that success isn't how much money you make or how big your business is; it's the freedom to do whatever you want with your time. Many other CEOs are disconnecting online so they can connect better in other ways.

The late Karl Lagerfeld, fashion tech visionary, tycoon, and creative director at Chanel, said that he did not use a computer, and it was also reported that he claimed he didn't use a smartphone.[8] Simon

[6] https://www.usatoday.com/story/tech/2020/02/25/warren-buffett-finally-replaces-flip-phone-iphone/4866187002/
[7] https://www.huffpost.com/entry/mikhail-prokhorov-russian_n_583140
[8] https://www.wsj.com/articles/SB10657276093276200

Cowell, the man behind the world's most popular reality show, *American Idol*, does not use a computer, according to *Forbes* magazine[9].

The Supreme Court justices use memos instead of emails. Justice Elena Kagan said that the justices are not necessarily the most technologically sophisticated people.[10] CEOs tend to unplug from technology for the same reason. Sun Tzu, one of the greatest strategists ever, is quoted as saying, "Strategy without tactics is the slowest route to victory. Tactics without strategy is the noise before defeat."

Strategy is incredibly important in business, but there's a problem. Organization is not usually our greatest skill. However, CEOs and millionaires are masters at this. In-depth strategy and planning is something they don't put off.

Dan Henry heavily researched this topic and found that online planners were too complicated. He described the planning apps on his computer and smartphone as the two biggest productivity killers ever invented. The constant calls, messages,

[9] https://www.forbes.com/2008/06/10/celebs-without-tech-tech-cx_ew_0611sanstech.html?sh=fdb65da4259e

[10] https://www.businessinsider.com/justice-kagan-reveals-that-the-supreme-court-is-totally-technologically-challenged-2013-8

notifications, and interruptions made it impossible to get anything important done.

When I read this in his book *Plan Tomorrow*, I thought to myself: *We like to think we're hard at work, but oftentimes we are hardly working.*

Dan divulged his precious personal secret: "I happened to see an interview with Barbara Corcoran, one of the panelists on the *Shark Tank*. She mentioned that she followed the ABC method of prioritizing, based on the idea that your tasks should be categorized into the things A) you must do, B) the things you should do but aren't urgent, and C) the things that would be nice to do if you had the time."

Look at the interruptions digital media has created in our lives. A teacher, Julie Holland Griggs, posted this on Facebook on April 13, 2021:

> "In preparation for reading *Fahrenheit 451*, my class did a little social experiment today. While they were working at their desks, I had them quietly move to the board and make a tally mark each time they got a notification on their phone. Grand total for today: 1,687 notifications.

That's 1,687 interruptions to learning caused by cell phones. One of the central ideas of *F451* is that constant, mindless distractions prevent people from developing authentic relationships and suppress deep thought. Hmmm ..."

From Julie Holland Griggs's Facebook post (included with permission)

When we can't get away from our smartphones and we are depending on them during every waking moment, this has in essence become an addiction.

Do you believe it is a necessary strategy to take breaks from technology as a powerful concept that will allow you to transform your life and become more filled with the invisible things in life?

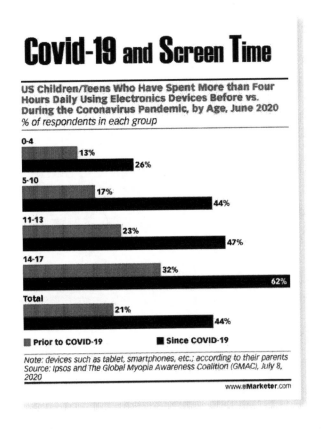

In this online age, the personal computer is a way of connecting to the world, but haven't we become more personally disconnected than ever before? Human connection is what fuels our souls. The impersonal technological gadgets to which we have become addicted to are robbing our souls. Ideally, what should fill us in marketing to the point of overflowing is inspiration and creativity, and that comes from an invisible source and not a digital device.

Ask yourself one question: would Jesus Christ have had a cell phone? If He had, would He call you, or would He just text you? I have my own thoughts on this, but I'll let you ponder it for a while.

Famous CEOs are leading us to understand that online interactions are a far cry from having deep personal relationships. Killing It Online has a mission beyond featuring people who do well in online business. Moreover, this is a movement that teaches us how to connect with the meaningful things in life because this is what gives us true fulfillment.

In my humble opinion, the biggest change from the yellow page era is that we have to a great degree lost the ability to connect personally. My contention is that technology has turned everything into a process. Look at the effects that COVID-19 has had on the use of our devices. I don't even know where to start in understanding how it has changed our relationship with God.

Now that you know more about Google and smartphones, and why I struggled with the changes of technology, let's go back to where I was at with my "Rock Bottom Reality Check!"

GOING FROM LOST TO FOUND

After I decided to leave my yellow page job and plunge into my new career, it seemed like a good idea to relocate to a major market of California. I thought it would be a great place to get immersed in the digital world. Everything had deteriorated in just a couple of months since I'd left the wilds of North Idaho. I even took a job selling ads on the backside of grocery store receipts, which was harder than hawking ads in the back of phone books. Transitioning into a digital world wasn't as easy as I thought.

California was an entirely different animal from what I had expected. The sophistication in marketing was a quantum leap from where I had been. I had great success with my past marketing accomplishments, but now it was a whole new world. Marketing agencies were not very interested in talking to me. Really, what could an ex-yellow page salesman offer them? My varied types of messages to them remained unreturned and my emails were never opened. What does it take to be an expert in today's online domain? My thoughts were hopeful, but I was preoccupied with memories of success from the past.

This experience was life-changing because I faced a lot of situations where I had to decide whether to pursue the world or a more spiritual life. Living in Southern California seemed to be all about keeping up appearances, and the thought of retiring there on the income of a former yellow page salesman was completely daunting.

I stayed in Pasadena for three months, but I found that it was just too expensive, and I decided to move to San Diego. I found a reasonable place to live for about one-third of what I had been paying. Even so, I spent all my savings from my yellow page years because I had ridden the yellow pages bus for too long. After eight months in San Diego, I got down to my back against a wall. There is no greater stress than when you have a ticking clock, and the money has run out. I know this feeling of dread very well.

At that time, I noticed that there were a lot of homeless people where I was living in San Diego. I decided to start making friends with them because I thought I could possibly end up in a situation like theirs, someday soon. One problem with being poor is that you don't have a lot of options and you have to be really good at managing finances. I needed to rebuild my life, and suicide wasn't an option because I don't believe in giving up. To me, life is all about the comeback story.

Since my car kept overheating, I couldn't work and had to wait a week for my new credit cards to arrive. Like I said before, the only job I could find worth anything was working for a company called Register Tape, where we sold advertising on the back of grocery store receipts. That was the toughest sales gig I think I've ever had in my life. I was making seventy to eighty cold calls a day and was barely making it.

As I mentioned before, when I lost my wallet, I had my come-to-Jesus moment. While sitting at my desk, a lightbulb went off in my head! I remembered the day I moved into my high-rise condo that had a view of the waterfront. However, since it overlooked the shipyards, it was in an area of town that most people considered highly undesirable: National City, California. I remembered it was New Year's Day and I had eaten a delicious steak and lobster dinner right across the street from my new place. It was a great meal for a reasonable price. It was during this remembrance that an idea popped into my head about where I could get my next meal.

I decided to walk across the street and ask to speak with the restaurant owner. The idea began to take shape and become much clearer to me. His nightclub/restaurant didn't look the greatest on the outside but was decent inside and had delicious food at affordable prices. I believed it would appeal to a lot more people if they knew what it looked like on the inside.

I had enough money for a beverage, but food was a gamble. I had watched people driving by this restaurant and it seemed they were not willing to stop. My idea was to feature one really good photograph of how appealing the interior of his restaurant was and post it on the biggest search engine on the planet, Google. We could also place it on other social media platforms. The owner, who was usually absent, just happened to be there, and he and I ended up "gifting" him my services for a nice dinner. I was confident that I could help him, like I had helped so many of my past yellow page customers, especially with this inspiration that I believed was from God.

They say a picture is worth a thousand words, but in this case, for McDini's restaurant, it was worth a lot more! I posted the picture and an honest review, and it went on to harvest more than one million views on Google. The vision had been true! People really wanted to take a digital look at this restaurant before stepping inside. Thinking about this, I began to see how I could go to the surrounding businesses and offer my services, taking them from lost to found and then to overflowing with business. So it was ironic that I seemed to be going from a point of lost to found in my own personal life.

Not long after this, my stay in San Diego was cut short when I found that my car was on its last legs. Having practically nothing, I felt a desire to turn my chaos into order. This was when I decided to press the reset button in my life, leaving California. My greatest fear was seeing my life deteriorate in front of me, and I did not want to be dependent on somebody else.

A DEFINING MOMENT FOR THE DIGITAL REVOLUTION

Looking back, I begin to see how I'd gotten into this predicament. It was the first Tuesday of November in 2008, the day of President Barack Obama's election. It was a defining moment in our history, and Americans were hungry for change, but I was not prepared for the looming changes ahead. In retrospect, it was another one of the worst days of my life.

In reality, it was the first nail in the coffin for the "Death of a Yellow Page Salesman." Like Willy Loman, I had gone back to what was familiar and secure, unwilling to make the change after an initial success with an online venture several years before.

Three years earlier, in 2005 when I was in Arizona, I went through a transition when our biggest competitor, YellowBook, bought our company out. Our company, TransWestern Publishing, with 380 telephone directories, was the largest independent yellow pages publisher in the nation and was very much a dominant force in the industry. Non-phone company books were known as independents, and we were a thorn in the side of YellowBook.

Our sales teams had been setting records across the country because of some unique training we had implemented. YellowBook paid an incredible amount of money for our company. They were buying out their largest competitor. Typically, you pay two times the annual net profits to buy a business, but they paid multiple times what we were worth.

They sat us all down after the merger. I had been a training manager, and I had trained quite a few sales teams over the previous three years. My new YellowBook managers told me, "You're not going to be a manager anymore. What we will do is make you a salesperson since you're so good at selling new business. You sold more new business than anybody even while managing a team. So, if you sell twice as much new business as last year, you'll make the same income you did before." I declined the offer and took a sales management position with AutoMart, the sister company to AutoTrader.com, thinking it was the perfect time for me to break into digital media sales.

I single-handedly launched us in the Tucson market, which had just under a million people. In my first six months I became the #1 small market representative in the nation for AutoMart. At this time, cars were the second-most searched-for items on the internet. I found the experience meaningful because I really began to understand the power of Google. We had been "Killing It with Google" for several years and were generating more than 160 leads per dealer. The average cost of $7 a lead was unheard of.

After a year, I noticed that all of a sudden, the number of leads from our website dropped by half. I thought there had to be something wrong with our website. After investigating, our web team said every-thing was fine. It was scary to realize that people were just not searching for cars like they used to. In my gut, it felt like the ship was taking on water and we were already sinking. In reality, the recession was starting to show its ugly head.

Even though I didn't know what was happening, I knew that I needed to do something different. At about this time, I was sitting at my desk wondering what I was going to do. It was precisely then that I

received a phone call from my old yellow page directories boss, Bart. With a rapidly contracting automotive market, I was grateful for this well-timed
phone call. Bart and I had worked together on and
off for about five years in yellow pages, setting many
sales records.

He asked me if I was interested in helping him build
a sales team for Phone Directories Company (PDC),
which was located in twenty markets in Arizona. He
then told me that I was his first call, and I was honored
that he wanted to develop a sales team around me. If
I agreed to the arrangement, he explained, I would be
the recruiter and sales trainer, supervising a group of
sixty reps. At the time, they had ten representatives,
and we needed to ramp up in just a few months with
fifty more. The publishing firm we would be working for had acquired a small Utah yellow pages firm
and was the former CanPages of Canada. They were
more established in Canada than Google.

Wow, I thought. Here I was in an incredible position where we were "Killing It with Google" with
AutoMart, but I was considering going back to work
with the yellow pages. With my responsibilities, I
opted for what I thought was solid security. Long
story short, I accepted the position with Bart because
of the economy's uncertainty.

We quickly increased to the sixty-rep threshold and sales began to take off. During this time, I taught the reps how to go in and help small business owners, not only with traditional advertising but also with digital aspects, such as by using Google, Facebook, and other online media. We offered packages to help our traditional yellow page clients by catering to their digital needs. We specialized in driving better-converting online leads, whether through building websites, managing online listings, or even creating videos and SEO packages.

With this opportunity, I believed that the silver lining would be working in the digital market using this traditional base. I could see that the old tradition was rapidly going digital, and millions of businesses would soon need help to make the switch from old school to 2.0!

My philosophy for my team was that we would have fun while making a lot of money. This was by far the most rewarding experience of my career. I saw the growth in the new reps and how they could effect change not only in the small business owners' lives but also in their own. We only lost four reps out of the fifty in our first year. This was unheard of, especially in our sales industry that normally averaged a 30 percent attrition rate. Meanwhile, Google was beginning to dominate in an incredibly aggressive fashion.

However, that good year was short-lived and changed the day Obama was elected. The entire sales staff was called together with all of our state and regional managers. The whole sales team thought and anticipated that I was going to be promoted to a manager. Unexpectedly, we were told in the first few minutes that we needed to pack up all of our things and had two hours to be out of the office. Everyone was completely stunned and devastated! The next day, as reality began to set in, I received twenty-eight phone calls from all of my close reps asking me what I was going to do. At the time, I didn't know the answer, but I knew that I would need to find something to support my family and then transfer completely to online marketing.

Me and Tommy-Boy,
my traveling companion

Being that it was 2008, I didn't expect I would be doing piecemeal work until the same company hired me back. Instead of working in Arizona, I had transferred to work for PDC in Idaho and Montana. They told me that my income would start at a third of what I had made before but that I could work my way back up to become a sales trainer. For two weeks I settled back into the routine of being just a salesperson, and then I had an unexpected surprise.

My job was 3.5 hours east of my home in North Idaho, so I would leave on Monday morning and get back Friday afternoon. I had put our large Dodge Ram truck up for sale because I had fallen behind on my payments, even though I carried all my bills for over a year with little to no income.

I was on my way home Friday when a young man rammed the rear end of my full-size truck at 50 miles per hour. He totaled his truck. My foot was on the gas, so when he hit me, the impact shoved my foot all the way down to the floor boards and my truck shot forward with such an explosive force it felt like I was being shot out of a cannon. I will never forget it.

When it happened, I thought it was all over, but luckily, I survived it. If I had been in my Volkswagen Bug, I would have been dead. My recovery from a serious back injury went on for a year and a half, and I couldn't work or drive much at all. This completely wiped us out financially, and afterward all of our savings and our home were gone. I thought this was the final nail in the coffin of my yellow page career.

What I didn't expect was that my wife would leave me without any explanation. It was a simple email two months after she left that read, "I have decided to not continue on in the marriage." That is when I became totally lost and everything was impacted by me viewing myself as a victim. In retrospect, I realized that I had been struggling with this mentality from 2010 to 2017.

Struggling as an unsuccessful person is not an empowered position, and it also leaves you all alone with nothing but self-pity. With this comes problems and frustrations. You feel like a victim and the world is against you. What is the key to getting on top of a situation like this? Nobody wants to end up like Willy Loman.

Less than two months ago, while on a 21-day vacation, I was able to share a brief version of my life with a man named Frank Casperson. After listening, he said, "You know, Paul, you are a never-say-die guy!"

LEAVING THE PAST BEHIND

Going back to the original story, to regain perspective, I left California, with my car on its last legs. I had friends in Boise, Idaho, and went to visit them. When I went to church, one of the leaders burst out, "Hey

Paul, why don't you move to Boise?" I thought, *That's not such a bad idea!*

I was absolutely lost at this point in my life, and I needed to get back on my feet. My best friend Matthew lived in Boise, and I visited him every time I passed through. He is a counselor, and we had known each other for a long time. Matthew and I had this natural kinship, and we liked hanging out together. We always picked up right where we left off the last time we'd seen each other. Getting up the courage, I asked him, "Hey Brother, what do you think if I stayed with you for a while?" He responded, "Absolutely—my son David recently moved out and I have an empty bedroom, so yes, it would be great."

During my time there, I decided the best thing I could do was pray and heal and ask God for a good job and a fresh start. In a simple prayer, I asked the Lord for a job in marketing where I could really help make a difference for a nonprofit or Christian group. The first response to my prayer that I saw occurred in a conversation I happened to have with a monk, and that was what led to my going into a monastery in Virginia becoming a possibility. I began to realize I was more broken than I thought and that I needed to work on myself. Many times, I have heard people say that monasteries are hospitals for the soul. It is true;

they are a place to heal and to grow, but the experience is not easy. I knew I needed to work on myself, and the monastery seemed like the place to do it.

Me with a young visitor who came with her
grandmother to the monastery

TIME IN THE MONASTERY

As far as how I felt in the monastery, it was a spiritually intense time when I felt empty, but I was being filled. Monks who have written about living in monasteries have said it is a time where you are essentially alone with God, and boy was that true. When you are living in quiet and solitude, you have time for God to do major construction on your life. Spending hours on end every day contemplating my life led me to wanting to get back to living like they did in the Book of Acts. This quote below by Elder Ephraim describes what happened to me." [11]

Monasticism is a free hospital, a hospital of God, where a person comes to feel better. God calls on a person with His holy call and with His love leads him into this free medical clinic.

A person seeks healing and cries: "Lord Jesus Christ, have mercy on me." "Yes, I will have mercy on you," answers the Lord. So, the physician of our souls and bodies proceeds to healing.

He sends us various sorrows, allows temptations. And all this is a bitter medicine curing the human soul.

Elder Ephraim of Arizona

However, while I was at the monastery, I had a lot of time to reflect on the things that I had learned previously and strengths I had developed in my life. The paradox was that my greatest strengths were what I struggled most with now.

---

[11] https://en.m.wikipedia.org/wiki/Ephraim_of_Arizona

Because of my own dilemmas and fears, my mindset had changed from the one that I had developed through my career and also from my youth. Bear with me as I share some of my reflections because I learned a lot from my contemplations at the monastery, and I believe some of it will help others.

THE TWO DIFFERENT MINDSETS

There is an incredible power in words, and choosing the right words in marketing can make all the difference to the success of a campaign. It is important to have the right mindset; this determines a lot about where some goes in life.

Remembering back, I learned a great lesson about this from Jay Mitchell, Vice President of Franchising for U-Save Auto Rental. This was a firm I worked for when I took a break from the yellow pages, right before the tragedy of September 11, 2001. Jay taught me to look for one of two mindsets in people. People of one mindset look for reasons they should do something. What they are actually looking for is validation. For example, they would call and say they are really interested in knowing more about buying a franchise and ask how they can benefit from it. And the second group has in mind all their objections and they question why they should even think about doing it. This became a discourse to prove to them that they should buy.

Jay told me to only work with people who have the positive mindset. This was revolutionary to me, and it somewhat rubbed me the wrong way, but I found that I could discover people's mindset by listening to their first few sentences when they spoke. For example, somebody would call me up and ask, "Why should I buy this franchise? It seems like you charge a lot for something I could do myself." I would answer, "You don't seem to see the value in buying a franchise and until you do, I don't think we have a lot to talk about." It is hard enough in life to keep your own thoughts positive, but when you limit what you accept from others it becomes easier. It is amazing to learn so much about your own mind in the quietude of a monastery.

TOP GUN TRAINING—THE IMPORTANCE OF COMMUNICATION

Thinking about my past, when I was twenty years into my sales career in 1999, I went through some of the greatest sales training ever. This is when I learned the art of effective communication. It was called

Top Gun Sales Training, under a trainer named Matt Wells. During this time, I was in yellow page sales, and this session completely transformed my career and my life.

When the going got tough, it was this training that helped me to understand what I needed by saying it out loud. I began to use this knowledge to find my life again.

I remembered from the training that Matt had actually instructed top gun fighter pilots—people who are all about processes and safety. Regarding his experience, Matt said, "If you're flying in formation at Mach I, and you're wing tip to wing tip, you have to know how to communicate effectively. You also need to know what's in the mind of the other pilot." For instance, if they say bank to 45 degrees and head 180, both of you need to know what is in the mind of the other person; this is effective communication.

Our instructor also taught us that people only listen to 9 percent of what a salesman says. Salesmen like to talk, talk, talk, but that's not necessarily the best way to connect. In the training, Matt emphasized that words are very powerful. Keeping this in mind, if you key in and really listen to what people say, you can find out what's motivating them to take action or why they're even interested in talking to you.

Then he went on to say, "The real key is connecting with the customer. So, when you listen to them and you repeat back what they say by mentioning, 'That's interesting what you said about this. Let me know a little bit more about that.' When you do this, you connect with them and begin to learn what is in the mind of the customer, and the customer appreciates your interest."

When Matt was talking about this, he blew my mind. After that session, I learned that marketing is a matter of connecting with the customer—a little like developing a romantic relationship. And I said to myself, *What?*

In marketing, you can't simply go through the motions. In contrast, many of today's youth treat work like a routine process. For instance, a Fortune 100 retail company I worked with struggled with training youth. In response, I told them, when we look at some of the salespeople in their twenties and early thirties, we find that they mainly emphasize efficiency and work entirely within a system and a framework of process.

However, a woman in her forties at this retail company operated differently because she strove to make personal connections with her customers. She ended up among the top five in the region in four categories for sales. This was top-gun training in action, and I wanted to make her an example. She sold the same way I have always done, by bonding and establishing a personal connection.

As you can see, the key is really to relate by asking the right questions. She communicated in a completely different, more personal way than did her peers. When you ask targeted questions, people are more engaged. When I talked with her, I asked her if people asked specifically to work with her. She said, "There are a lot of people who want to work with me, just because I show interest in solving their problems."

Even in the small things that we do, we should not just focus on the process. For instance, if you are cold and visibly systematic in your dealings, then it becomes an impersonal encounter. Conversely, when you are warm and genuinely concerned, the individual becomes very special to you. This is one of the things I love about sales work—people respond when you show empathy and care.

CHANGE THE MESSAGING

When I was at the monastery, I was partnered with a nonprofit group that works with Christian mission groups in Africa, and it was an incredibly rich experience.

The first thing I did for the nonprofit was write an article for one of their missions. I noticed that they were talking about the fact that they had almost 200 kids and that they needed about $200 a day to feed and house the children.

I thought to myself, that is only a dollar a day, so I changed the message for their entire campaign: "For only a dollar a day, you can help change the life of a child." The donations to the missions using this message went up noticeably. This emphasizes that your core message in your marketing is everything. Before I share other principles about what makes marketing effective, let me continue with my story.

A local priest with
a child and me

After changing the message for the African missions, things took off and I actually ended up going to Africa for most of the next summer. I visited close to forty different mission groups. I spent a week in each area and traveled with some of the area priests, pastors, and mission directors. We really liked to work with orphanages and schools because of the work they did with the children. Helping to start several orphanages was a life-changing experience. It seemed like my life was taking on new meaning as I was giving and benefiting others with my marketing and business experience. The promise God had made to me at Jacob's Well was beginning to come to pass.

When I go out to speak at churches, I like to tell people what I learned from working with the leaders in Africa and the challenges they face. The Lord has helped me to inspire them and make positive changes for the future.

When I was in Kenya and Uganda making videos, coordinating the online marketing, and documenting the mission work, God inspired me to change the message of several of our missions for the next year. I changed it to "Look at the difference your donations have made." I began to document that we had constructed several buildings, bought land, and dug wells. These wells are called boreholes there because they are 900 feet deep and drilling them is like drilling for oil. These life-giving boreholes cost almost ten times as much to drill as wells in the United States. We also helped start three brand-new orphanages and several mission schools.

There was something important we had built: relationships and philanthropy. Often, missions from America are built on the idea of U.S. citizens being givers. The missions I was working with were sharing pictures, but they lacked story and context. We were teaching them that philanthropy was a relationship and not just a plea for donations. Ultimately, this was about distancing themselves from simply blurting out their dire needs. Before, the messaging hadn't been focused and it didn't personally relate. I imagined people who saw these posts might think, "Yes, we know you have this need and we know of your pleas, but would you stop begging?"

Begging is distasteful; however, after seeing it firsthand and having experienced how pervasive poverty is, then you begin to understand why people beg. When you haven't had anything substantial to eat and you have food only three times in a week, anything is worth the risk. Even a person's pride is thrown away to survive.

When I was in Africa, I was impressed with one particular Bible verse, and I didn't understand why God had laid it on my heart. I had tried to remember it because my laptop wasn't working very well in rural Kenya, but it was the verse that says you always have the poor with you. It haunted me because it seemed like an excuse to not give to the poor. Like, what is the use? They will always be here begging.

I could not get that verse out of my mind for over a week, and it finally came to me where the great commission is in Matthew 25 and 26. I finally looked it up because it was so relentless. When I found it, I was only thinking about the first part of the verse spoken by Jesus: *The poor you'll always have with you, but you will not always have me.* —Matthew 26:11 (KJV)[12]

Then the verse began to make sense to me. I thought, as poor as the Kenyans and Ugandans were financially, they still had Jesus. Compared to us in the United States, they had praise and worship like I had never seen before. They were poor, but I thought, *Who are the poor ones? Them, or us?*

I thought about myself—how poor I was, not only financially but also spiritually, desiring to be filled. Several months before I wanted to see if the monastery was something that would interest me, I flew out to the D.C. area and spoke with a man of God for five days. He heard my life story, and I was very

---

[12] https://www.kingjamesbibleonline.org/Matthew-26-11/

drawn to him. My desire was to heal and pick up the pieces of my life and I wondered where we went from there. I didn't know if I had the makings of a monk. I have always thought of monks as being quiet, which isn't me. I'm very talkative and very energetic. The abbot told me, "No, you'd be exciting to be around." This was when my focus and mission in life solidified to help those who desire to share the Gospel and help them in a time of need with their messaging and marketing.

HONEST COMMUNICATION

My father

My father was a pastor who worked with alcoholics and drug addicts. He started three very successful treatment centers in the Midwest. One of the things he taught is that if you really want to know yourself, don't look at yourself in the mirror.

If you really want to know how you come across to others, get the five people closest to you and ask them to honestly answer this question: "How do I come across to you, and how do I make you feel?" This will help you know whether you are warm and empathetic, or if you come across in a way that might surprise you.

Honest communication is such a powerful experience because when you understand how to motivate and inspire people, you will become very popular and well liked. To be effective with people, you need to deliver your personal messaging in a clear way. I had learned all these things, but why couldn't I apply them to my own life? Sometimes, when a person goes through severe loss, it stops being a matter of what you know and becomes one of how you start to overcome your loss. Fear of failure is an incredible barrier in life. Willy Loman never got a handle on this. I didn't want to end up like him in the final act of *Death of a Salesman*.

Salespeople like to think of themselves as master communicators, but reality can get distorted by things like denial and the inability to break free from the past and move into the future. Change is sometimes the toughest thing we can accomplish. That is when we need to learn to move forward in our lives, when it seems like we are stuck and can't move.

Like Willy Loman, I struggled with the past and was not embracing the future, especially as it led to so many new changes. For example, Google and online marketing were blazing a trail with technology that was completely taking over the business world. Coming back from this was difficult, to say the least. The problem was that I didn't know I was lost, but I finally realized I was drowning in fear, and what I mostly drew strength from were the lessons I learned when I was growing up.

There is no fear in love; but perfect love casts out fear . . . But he who fears has not been made perfect in love.
—1 John 4:18 (New KJV)[13]

PERSPECTIVE IS EVERYTHING

Losing your perspective in life is somewhat like being lost at sea. Not knowing where you are, especially if you try to act like you do, ultimately gives you a gnawing feeling that you are becoming even more lost. One of the unique advantages of being lost at sea in a large sailboat is that you can change your

---

[13] https://dailyverses.net/1-john/4/18/nkjv

perspective and get your bearings by climbing the mast. This is where taking on a perspective other than your current one can have a powerful influence on your dilemma. If you have ever experienced sheer panic, you will know that once you fully realize you're lost, you know the feeling of terror or dread. Now we

Climbing will certainly change your perspective.
Photo credit: Pixabay

have the clear advantage of numerous electronic navigational devices, but what if you did not?

The best advice I have ever heard is that if you are not sure about something in your gut, don't do it. The night before I have to make a big decision, if I cannot sleep and I know there is something I am not comfortable with, I put it on the shelf for at least a night and maybe longer. When I wake up with an assurance about it, then I believe it is settled.

Consulting a perspective other than your own can change everything.

When I found myself lost because of the final demise of my occupation, my focus was on the negative, and all I could see was the lack in everything:

Lack of accomplishments	Lack of fun
Lack of confidence	Lack of connection
Lack of focus	Lack of caring
Lack of positive self-talk	Lack of peace
Lack of boldness	Lack of order
Lack of friends	Lack of favor

One of the most popular verses of all time is *As a man thinketh in his heart, so is he.* —Proverbs 23:7 (KJV)[14]

How devastating is loneliness and feeling like you're a failure, losing the admiration of your family and friends and loved ones? Friends don't want to hang out with you as much. People don't return your calls. You feel alone and rejected. Your hopes of enjoying life and experiencing success are all things of the past because the world has moved on without you. You have been left behind. Life is an uphill effort all the time. You are outside instead of inside. You have lost the respect of those closest to you.

---

[14] https://www.kingjamesbibleonline.org/Proverbs-23-7/

At this time in my life, I thought this was caused by the advancement of technology, and I felt the whole world was against me. You don't want to feel like a victim, but you do. How do you overcome a cycle of defeat when your mind has overtaken you and there doesn't seem to be any way out? The problem with a victim mentality is that you are not empowered to overcome your circumstances.

"For I know the plans I have for you, declares the Lord,.."
Jeremiah 29:11 (NIV)
Image by Benjamin Balazs-Pixabay

So, the question is, how do you come back from such a point of emptiness when you have lost everything and feel abandoned? How do you create meaning for your own life in a shallow and empty world? A world where everything has gone from personal and intimate to callous and insensitive stops you from living a life that is filled to overflowing. It really comes down to a process of transformation.

In the book *How Are You Scripting Your Life?* author Ene I. Ette writes, "Your tongue/mouth sets the direction for the course of your life. You can use your tongue to transform your life for good or bad. The choice is yours."[15] It was providential when I met Dr. Ette in church, and in the first five minutes of his presentation he gave me his book. The promise he made me pledge is that I would use his book. God must have told him something.

Ette writes, "Whether you know it or not, your words define you. They set a trajectory for your life. Thus, you use your words to write the script of your life."

The tongue can be an unruly evil. Proverbs 18:21 (KJV) says it this way: *Death and life are in the power of the tongue: and they that love it shall eat the fruit thereof.*[16] Your spoken words can speak life, or they can speak death. We have to bridle our tongues like horses and make them say what we want for our

15 Ene I. Ette, PhD, *How Are You Scripting Your Life?* Alaythace
16 https://www.kingjamesbible.me/Proverbs-18-21/

lives—not what we don't want. Before this passage, in Verse 20, it says, *A man's belly shall be satisfied with the fruit of his mouth; and with the increase of his lips shall he be filled.*[17] Our spirit within us is our belly, and when it is satisfied, all the meanings of life are derived from it.

"To know how you got to where you are now, check what you have been speaking over yourself. Yes, words do matter, and you should not take them lightly," Dr. Ette writes.[18]

THE POWER OF THE SPOKEN WORD

I learned the power of the spoken word very early on when I was working in Christian radio. There was a pastor who would come into the station every Friday to record his weekly broadcast. He was the director of the rescue mission in Salina, Kansas. We would talk every time he came in, and one time he said, "Paul, you should come and preach at the rescue mission."

"You know, Pastor, I'm not a preacher," I told him. "I am just a salesman for the radio station."

---

[17] https://www.kingjamesbible.me/Proverbs-Chapter-18/#20
[18] Ene I. Ette, PhD, *How Are You Scripting Your Life?* Alaythace

"No, you should!" he insisted. "Well, at least you could come and share your testimony."

I told him I had never done that before, but he tried one last time.

"Well, isn't there anything you'd like to share?"

I asked, "Has anybody ever just come and read the Bible?"

And he said, "Yeah, why don't you come and do that?"

So, I selected quite a few verses from the Gospel of John which all pertained to love. About forty guys had to listen to an hour-long talk, which was normally preaching. Here I was going to read to them from the Gospel of John before they ate. I had somebody play an acoustic guitar as I read, *In the beginning was the Word, and the Word was with God, and the Word was God.*[19] You know how John starts.

It was interesting because some of the guys were laying their heads down; it was just really quiet and peaceful. You know it was kind of amazing when it was just the Word of God spoken. After about forty-five minutes the atmosphere had completely changed. There was something going on, but I couldn't put my finger on it. I saw they were still preparing the meal

---

[19] https://www.kingjamesbibleonline.org/John-1-1/

and I needed to fill fifteen minutes. I was thinking, *I don't want to preach*, and so I asked, "Is anybody hungry? If so, raise your hand!"

Many of them responded, "Yeah, let's eat!"

I immediately said, "I'm not talking about physical food. I'm asking, Who's hungry for God?" I continued, "If you're hungry for God, I want you to come up and talk with the pastor right now."

Three guys came forward and the pastor got all kinds of excited. He said, "In twenty-seven years of doing this, this is the first time somebody came in and just spoke the Word of God. This is amazing!"

After the meal, the director asked me if I would come back the next month and do it again. I said, "Sure!" I did the same thing, reading like before. When I asked if anyone was hungry for God, fifteen guys came forward. This was the power of the spoken Word of God, and it was revolutionary for me. This motivated me to do mission work for twenty-five years and help start more than twelve churches and several orphanages and missions in Africa.

Words have meanings, and knowing the right things to say at a precise moment can be life-changing. This "speaking engagement" made such an impression on me that I never forgot the power of words and especially the power and the effect of the spoken Word of God. Needless to say, all these memories helped me to fill my well again and gave me a renewed commitment to serve the Lord in even more meaningful ways.

After all these reflections, the question that remained was how I would overcome fear and make a comeback in my life. I wrestled with so many thoughts and self-misconceptions that my greatest enemies were the thoughts that wouldn't leave my mind. After almost two years at several monasteries, I felt it was time to start filling the emptiness I carried. What provided me with a strong foundation were all the people I had helped with their marketing and advertising campaigns. My real forte was in making their messaging and communication effective and creating momentum for their businesses.

PART II

PRINCIPLES OF MOMENTUM — FILLING THE WELL

IN THE FIRST section, you read about going from lost to found, which is knowing where you are in life and beginning to take action so you can grow. Here in the second section, I talk about creating and building momentum, how important the words we say are, and how critical messaging is. Messaging isn't just about things that you hear and think about; it's also about going beyond contemplation to become a doer and not just a hearer. To be guided and directed by God, you must first be moving. I remember teaching my young children to ride bicycles. They couldn't learn anything until they were moving. When we realize this, we understand how creating momentum can be the beginning of a turnaround. This section is focused on moving forward.

One of the best marketing examples for this was when I put an Iowa massage therapist, Denny McFadden, on the map with Google a few years ago. He had zero presence online, no website, just his personal cell phone and a license for massage. All he wanted was a presence on Google and a website. In his first month he received fifty-five views and three website visits. The website was built, but since he didn't want any search engine optimization (SEO) or review marketing done, the number stayed relatively small. So, it's one thing to have a presence and be found, but it is another to be able to capture traffic and fill your tank with lots of customers from online searches.

It has been four years since I created the Google listing below for Denny. He is currently ranked #56 on Google's local search for "Massage Therapy" at the time of printing. Let me explain the story further.

COMPETITION & MARKET CONDITION

Competitor Comparison		
Business	Ranking	Reviews
Iowa Massage Therapy (Avg 5.0)	#1	18
Massage Heights (Avg 4.3)	#2	71
Denny McFadden LMT (Avg 0)	#56	0

Remember the quote in the movie *Field of Dreams*: "If you build it, they will come"? However, in marketing, that's not true.

The point of learning this is that, like in the first section you read, Denny had gone from "lost to found," but he didn't put into practice the principles of "going from empty to filled." Now, I understand that fear and depression are the two greatest obstacles to overcome. The thing that died within me after my life working with the yellow pages was the confidence I used to have in myself. When this happened, I became stuck. I felt like the Dead Sea, and there was little to no life left in me! In effect, I had come to a grinding halt. My momentum had died.

LET'S GET DIGITAL—
THE NEW WORD-OF-MOUTH ADVERTISING

You may wonder whether I have a background in digital. Although I eventually became successful in the area, I did struggle when working for digital companies because when you have aged to your mid-fifties and early sixties as a former yellow page salesperson, your legitimacy, believability, and trust factors are diminished. People don't think you know anything about the internet. For example, when I interviewed with *AutoTrader*, I was almost sixty. They likely reasoned, "So, do you hire a guy who is sixty years old and a former yellow page salesman? He did pretty well with this company called Automart several years before."

How do you compare a young graduate, fresh out of college with a degree, to a sixty-year-old? The fresh graduates have the energy level of a rolling freight train, but their momentum is focused more on effort than effectiveness. Working smarter is always better than just working hard.

One thing I had done in the past which set me apart from recent graduates was founding an internet company called CaReport in 1995. At that time, there were only five different firms in the nation that had put databases of auto dealer inventories online. My business was located in the Pacific Northwest, and I had put thirty dealerships online with all of their inventories. My son Chris and I were working with Microsoft Access for the launch and, in my opinion, it is the worst database program ever written. However, I decided that the day Microsoft Windows 95 launched was the day I wanted to have our company's grand opening.

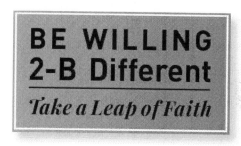

BE WILLING
2-B Different
Take a Leap of Faith

During the mid-'90s, the data transfer rates were only running at 300 bits per second. Now we're at 100 to 300 megabytes per second. Yes, we're talking about 100 million bits of information versus 300 bits. Initially, it was painfully slow. It used to take almost two minutes to download a one-megabyte picture of a car. My company was definitely far ahead of the curve—not digitally, but with its marketing innovations.

It was then that a light went on in my head. (Yes, I mean God!) I decided that we needed to change the message delivery system from the internet to a traditional one. This is because there were thought to be only 5 percent of the public online at that time. So, I advertised all over the Pacific Northwest in several small shopper newspapers, such as *Penny's Worth* and *Nickel Niks*. The ads were displayed in more than four million papers, saying, "You can find 30,000 Cars & Trucks in the Pacific Northwest in the CAReport. Just call this toll-free number for FREE information. We can send it directly to you for a small charge, or the dealership can contact you directly for FREE!"

A year and a half later, my largest client with three thousand vehicles asked, "How much would it be to just buy your entire business?" I threw out an incredibly high number, and they immediately jumped on it. Then they said, "You need to work with us for three months to teach us your system."

During that time in the mid-'90s, I taught them how to convert leads to sales by leaving the right information and having the prospective customers write the salesperson's name on something they keep right next to the phone. Yes, I know this was a technique I learned in my phonebook days.

Now, fast-forward ten years to when I worked for a sister company of AutoTrader. The power of AutoMart was that we had Google in the room when we designed our website. We asked the Google designers how we could dominate Google's organic listings. A lot of people don't know what that is, but it is software that creates a very searchable web address. The key is this one powerful thing: search-engine-friendly URLs.

At that point, the whole concept of "Killing It with Google" really came to me: how you can dominate and be in the top three in a Google search and also dominate all the free and the organic listings. Eventually, AutoMart was doing so well that AutoTrader bought us out.

Why were the yellow pages, and eventually Google, so incredibly effective?

When I started in the yellow pages in 1987, I learned a dynamic principle by observing the results of clients. Now mind you, that was way back then, but they still indicate the raw difference between marketing and advertising, and it still applies today.

We were taught in college that the average person is exposed to 3,800 advertising impressions per day. Of those, their minds consciously took in and recognized only a fraction of the messages. Do you know what fraction of those messages was recognized? Only 1 percent, which amounts to just forty advertising impressions. Of those ad impressions, an average of only four were acted upon. Conversely, at that time, 60 percent of people took action when they looked up a specific category in the yellow pages.

Clearly, there was a strong difference between advertising, which broadcasts to the masses, and marketing, which drills down to the specific niche or category. Now with internet marketing, you are able to drill down to the exact search of what you are looking for, allowing you to get results similar to what we saw in the yellow pages. However, when you spread the results over all the different venues available on the internet, it becomes much more of a challenge.

Advertising is an excellent means to build your brand, enhance top-of-mind awareness, and make the masses responsive to your business's product or service. Needs drive the search engine results.

Some of the most effective campaigns I have witnessed over the years have designed core messages and offers that dominated the market and positioned my clients as authorities. When you solve a problem with your messaging and focus your offer on people's needs, you will always get great results. Sometimes people will act to satisfy their wants, but their needs are what motivate them. This is the simplest but best advice I can give you.

As business and technology have changed through the years, these differences between marketing and advertising have blurred to the point that they seem the same, but they are not.

ADVERTISING VS. MARKETING

One of the main things I wanted to understand when I studied advertising and marketing at the University of Kansas was: What are the differences between marketing and advertising? Are they synonymous, or are they different? Sometimes words take on new meanings over the years. In this case, the meanings have changed dramatically. There is, however, a distinct difference between the two, so let me explain.

According to marketingprofs.com, "Advertising is just one component, or subset, of marketing. Public relations, media planning, product pricing and distribution, sales strategy, customer support, market research, and community involvement are all parts of comprehensive marketing efforts." However, because I view this in ways completely unlike these professors, I do differ from them in this approach. I believe they have made it a lot more sophisticated and technical in nature than it needs to be. Really, the concepts are simple in retrospect. Still, I do not think they are clear in people's minds.

As Kimberly McCall so aptly put it,

> *Marketing and advertising are fuzzy disciplines to begin with—ask 20 experts what the difference between the two is, and you'll get 20 diverse responses. Much of the business world stirs marketing and advertising together in one big bouillabaisse of methods to get products to prospects and clients. For professionals implementing marketing and advertising initiatives, however, it is important to understand that the terms are not synonymous.*[20]

---

[20] https://www.marketingprofs.com/authors/266/kimberly-mccall

Let me describe my view, which has always been that advertising is broadcasting your message to the masses, done mainly for wide-reaching campaigns when you want to touch every section of an audience. Things have become more niche these days, but back in simpler times, the most used advertising media were the newspapers, the local television stations, the local radio stations, and of course the yellow pages in the phone directories.

The complexity of options now, compared to then, is more perplexing, but understanding this very key element is the beginning of an effective advertising and marketing plan. The difference is the direction of your message: who it is directed at, and how are you able to deliver the message effectively to that specific audience?

A good analogy for this is if you were shooting with a rifle or with a shotgun. If you used a shotgun, it would blast in a short range with a very wide path, similar to what general advertising does. This is like trying to shoot your message to the masses. Conversely, if you take a rifle and zero in on your target, then it works as marketing does. It is a focused approach because you are precisely targeting your audience.

To recap, "shot-gunning it" is what advertising does. Marketing is when you take a rifle and zero in on your target, which is a much more defined capture, so to speak. Once you begin to implement this, momentum will develop, and it will seem like a cascading waterfall. This is when things become exciting for your business.

A waterfall of overflowing success
Image by Rudy and Peter Skitterians from Pixabay

Some of the stories from now on will relate my actual experiences from which I received inspiration that helped to develop momentum, to grow awareness and develop more customers. This knowledge and creative energy came from within and was from God. They had remarkable success. Through these stories, you can also discover how many have dominated and became the leaders of their industries.

THE POWER OF MOMENTUM

Momentum is very much like the movement of a loaded freight train. I grew up in the Midwest in Nebraska and Kansas, seeing trains from the Union Pacific railroad roll through our small town at 70 miles per hour. Because we couldn't cross the tracks with those trains rushing by, we had to travel by bus to school, so they had a very definite impact upon me.

If you have ever sat on a loaded coal train with 110 cars and waited 45 minutes to an hour for the brake test and brakemen to walk the train, you will understand the degree of patience required for an endeavor like this. Once the dispatcher gives the OK to move out onto the main line, the process of building momentum begins—the most difficult part.

Once the object is moving, it is easier to build up momentum. Through the years, I have seen business owners who had options but did absolutely nothing. This is when the advice to tackle the hardest thing first is met with great resistance. Start with something that will get you moving. Once you are moving, you will find it is easier to get more things done. This quote by George S. Patton, one of our nation's leaders, is really great advice: *"A good plan violently executed now is better than a perfect plan executed next week."*

SECRETS OF MARKETING EFFECTIVENESS

In this chapter, I share stories from a long time ago, and they make specific points I learned about marketing and also about myself. You will read specific case examples of clients I have worked with, helping to illustrate the principles of marketing effectiveness in a fun, easy-to-digest format. You can then understand the formula for success and what causes a campaign to cascade into a waterfall of overflowing success.

MAKE IT **FUN** & Simple	*Make it* Believable *-Connect w/ Others*	Promote what **U-Believe-'N** -BE FOCUSED

GET ONE THOUGHT *ACROSS* -HAVE CLARITY

Offer substance
that resonates & has meaning
-GREAT offers GET Results

MAKE MESSAGES *Shareable*

D E L I V E R **BOLDNESS!**

Be a Marketing GENIUS

Make Yourself Stand Out
-Be a Light in a Dark World

Dominate the Market!
-Grow a Loyal Following

ALLOW PROSPERITY **2-REIGN-N-U**

BE WILLING 2-B Different *Take a Leap of Faith*

Build 'N Maintain *MOMENTUM* -Offer GREAT Value

Be Real & Truthful
BECOME THE AUTHORITY

MAKE LIFE *Meaningful*

NeuStreams Media
MARKETING PRINCIPLES

KILLING IT ONLINE.COM

By Paul Neustrom - NeuStreams.com and KillingItOnline.com ©

GET ONE THOUGHT ACROSS (FOCUS)

Early on in my broadcast days, I was doing media consultation for a local bus company in Pullman, Washington. It was a small market of approximately 20,000 students and 12,000 residents. Although Washington State has grown immensely since this time, it was definitely what we called a "C-Market." Television wasn't a factor because it wasn't a cost-effective or viable option. We were an hour and twenty minutes away from Spokane, and was the closest TV market. However, when I brought up the idea of advertising on the radio, the company said immediately, "Oh, we tried that, and it didn't work."

Instead of asking what they tried and why it didn't work, I asked for more information with a positive approach: "What have you tried in the past in your other advertising, and why do you think that worked well for you?" Asking the question from this angle gave me some more insight, and it allowed me time to come up with an idea that could possibly work.

They mentioned that the best thing they had done was to print a two-page information guide in the student newspaper, which featured the schedules, routes, and prices. This was the only thing they were currently doing to promote themselves.

Then I learned that their funding was based entirely on semester-pass sales. This I would learn later was the "golden nugget."

That was when an idea popped into my head. I asked if they would be open to an idea I had. Instead of telling them what it was, I said they could listen to a demo spot or commercial I would make at our local radio station, KQQQ, which I was working with.

After going back to the broadcast studio, I spoke to our production manager, Jay, and told him about the idea I had for Pullman Transit. After discussing it for a short time, he arranged a spec spot, which had a parody of the Queen song "Another One Bites the Dust," called "Another One Rides the Bus" by Weird Al Yankovic. It also had sound effects of the bus doors closing and the deep bass sound of the exhaust as it took off. It was fun, and a very creative demo.

Typically, an effective campaign delivers a point of understanding that is not known in the market-place. In this case, people did not realize how inexpensive it was to ride the bus with a semester pass. So, the key to the success of this campaign was not just creativity but also the simple message. At the very end of the spot, Jay tagged it with: "For only $7.33 a month, another one rides the *bus!*" Little did

I know the effect that this campaign would have on this company and their newfound message.

The principle of getting one direct thought across has been a principle that through the years has been a resounding truth and is one of my greatest reasons for marketing and advertising effectiveness. So many times I have seen campaigns fail because they try to be too creative and don't emphasize this vital, straightforward marketing principle: G.O.T.A. (Get One Thought Across). I bet you thought I was going to say the K.I.S.S. method. Well, this parallels that too.

The bus company officials loved the demo commercial and decided to buy five 30-second radio ads a day. Because it was for their back-to-school promotion, the campaign was supposed to last for two weeks. Only three days into the campaign, they called me in a panic and said they needed to stop the ads. Bewildered, I asked them what had happened.

They excitedly told me, "We have completely run out of semester bus passes and need a few days to print more."

After resuming our back-to-school promotion, I encouraged them to buy fifteen commercials a day this time. I asked for some free bus passes, so we could give them away as prizes. We also threw in some live remote broadcasts when we could record riders of all types (not just students) and ask them why they were riding the bus. We got a lot of extra mileage from this, and it turned into a massive campaign. It was not only a successful promotion for our client, Pullman Transit, but also for the Hit Radio station itself. The one thing they had not anticipated was the overflowing thrust from word-of-mouth advertising. People discovered the most affordable deal on campus, and word spread like wildfire that they could ride the bus for next to nothing by getting a semester bus pass.

After having a lot of fun with the promotion and pounding the airwaves with commercials, the company asked for me to come in so that they could share the results with me. After we discussed how the campaign began and ended, they filled me in on the results of the Another One Rides the Bus campaign.

The results were so far beyond what they had expected that they changed their initial impulse against buying radio ads. What spoke to them the most (and this was back in the mid-1980s) was how the success had dramatically affected their budget based on the semester-pass sales, which appropriates funds for their new equipment budget. Remember that semester-pass sales determine their funding, which was their golden nugget.

With these new funds, they had amassed a budget big enough to pay for three brand-new buses, which were worth a total of $2.7 million, valued in 2022 dollars.

MAKE IT BELIEVABLE (INTENTION)

Another story is about a furniture liquidator that came to Spokane, Washington, to conduct a going-out-of-business sale for a prominent store. This store had a history of faithfully serving the Inland Pacific Northwest since 1925 and had a great reputation. With such a longstanding and excellent history of customer service and value, the owners said the closing sale had to be not only ethical and well regarded but also profitable.

The media buyer for the liquidators called all forty radio stations in the area, asking each station's sales rep to be at their office the following day with their best offers at 2 p.m. The next day, I prepared myself and purposely waited until I was last in line. I noticed that almost all the reps were dressed the same, the men mostly in blue blazers, white shirts, and red ties, and the women in nice suits. Because it took several hours to whittle down to the end, I went in without a blazer but had a colorful tie. I rolled up the sleeves on my pinstripe shirt and told them I had excellent news for them: "I am the last person you are seeing today, and I believe we have saved the best for last."

They looked at me kind of strangely for being so bold. I recited one of my favorite sayings, "I have an idea for you!" which had made me a lot of money throughout the years. I put it out there and said, "I have an idea for you, but if you want to do it, you will need to spend $10,000 in monthly billing with me throughout the entire campaign." These campaigns typically lasted three to six months.

When they asked who I worked for, I told them 96 Apple FM.

In response, they said, "You are ranked #10."

I said, "Yes, by the number of listeners in the average quarter-hour, but we have the largest cumulative audience. With this kind of spend, you will talk to more people—more often than other radio stations—by a large proportion."

They asked, "What is the idea?"

I then firmed up the $10,000 in monthly billing (the $10,000 in 1985 was equivalent in purchasing power to about $26,900 in 2022) and they told me that it was one-quarter of their entire budget. Then they said, "OK, we will do it if we have never done this idea before!"

I then threw it out there: "OK, gentlemen, have you ever tried, 'Name Your Own Price, with No Reasonable Offer Refused'?"

They responded, "Oh, we have done that several times before."

It was right then that an incredible thought came to me (yes, from God), and I believed it would make all the difference, but don't let me get ahead of myself. Most furniture liquidators use the same tired old message of "Save up to 70 percent off on our going-out-of-business sale," but nobody believes it!

Make it Believable

Making the message believable has the greatest potential to produce great results!

After coming back with that, I understood that they had tried this standard promo of name-your-own-price before, and I asked, "But have you ever tried it with actualities?" They looked puzzled, so I used a hypothetical example: "It would be something like this: Sally Smith came in from Walla Walla, Washington, and named her own price on an oak dining room set and six matching chairs, and out the door it went for $349."

The media buyer said, "I love it! Let's do it!"

I just love hearing these words!

It was the largest order in our station's history.

He did have me agree that our station would do the production for all of the other radio stations and provide the audio for the TV spots. So, once a week, I gathered their actualities. Over time, I became friends with the primary buyer.

At the end of the campaign, he invited me to come in, and they told me some exciting news. He said, "Of all the liquidation sales we have done, and we have done a lot of them, this was the first time we have never had to do an auction at the end." That was because they did not have enough leftover inventory to do one. He went on to say, "We are all going on a cruise, thanks to you, since we finished up three weeks early." Not only did this idea make a big impact on this promotion, but it also continued helping me effect change in many other campaigns after this.

When the message of a campaign is simple and believable, people get excited about sharing their experiences of naming their own prices—in this instance, the fantastic deals they received from Bell Furniture's final liquidation.

KNOW YOUR TARGET AUDIENCE (CONNECT)

One of the things that Spokane was known for is being one of the best test markets in the nation.

Because Spokane was a town of less than 500,000 people at the time, many believed that if you could get its residents to accept something, then you could gain acceptance nationally. In the past, many companies struggled to introduce new ideas that never gained traction.

Working as a consultant with the same radio station as in the previous story, word had spread about me and I was asked to consult with a new wireless company, Cellular One. They were in the test-market phase before launching their nationwide service. I was to advise them on campaign strategy, as they had just started the month before. A lot was riding on this campaign at that time.

In the mid-1980s, in the middle of winter, they had spent $100,000 in their first month but had only activated one hundred cellular phones. When you look at the customer acquisition cost per phone, there was no way that they could be successful at the rate of $1,000 per phone. It was cost-prohibitive, but at this point, they were willing to revamp their entire campaign strategy. Because they were in the proving grounds before the national launch, they wanted to know what could be done to gain traction in such a challenging market.

To identify what their strategy was, I posed the following question: "What do you believe is the most crucial benefit of your cellular phone to the general public?" Their response blew me away. They said, "Convenience." I was surprised and began to wonder who they thought their primary audience was. It did not seem to be directed toward women because if it were, it would be targeting an entirely different desire.

The needs of your prospect drive the marketing. Never forget that—needs absolutely drive marketing!

As they continued rambling on about how a phone provides convenience and flexibility and mobility and all that, I finally spoke up. "I don't believe the real need is convenience, although it may be a desire. I believe the best motive to promote is safety, because it targets the primary need people have, especially when they are in their car." I asked them to consider it from the vantage point of a woman.

They were absolutely stunned and reasoned that the best candidates for cellular phones were businesses because they were far more accessible for sales, rather than consumers, with less spending. At that point, the meeting could have gone south really fast, so I piped up with an idea I thought of right there on the spot.

-BE FOCUSED

I proposed that we needed to demonstrate the actual use of a phone, overheard on the radio, in an emergency. The concept involved using a recorded listener calling in to our radio station. This would be powerful because of the theater of the mind. It would not only demonstrate the benefit but also create a strong emotional desire for the product!

One of the real problems in Eastern Washington and Northern Idaho in the wintertime is black ice. The temperatures along Interstate 90, the main traffic corridor, hover right above freezing during most winter days and just below freezing at night.

My belief was that the primary concern of the general population was safety. Convenience factors in, yes, but it is more of a want or a desire. Knowing when there is black ice on the road would be of tremendous benefit to them.

I painted a picture like this: "Can you imagine someone calling in to the radio station on their cell phone and saying, 'I am right on I-90 at the state line, and there is a six-car pile-up. I am OK but just wanted to let everyone know that they should be careful and avoid this area at all costs!'" OK, I have a flair for the dramatic, but I wanted to demonstrate how the voice is the most persuasive medium, especially in a live broadcast.

Although we would first take the call live on the phone, we would broadcast the recording only once we had verified the report and informed the authorities. Audio is the most powerful of all media because it uses the human voice, as was witnessed by the results.

We said we would ask the radio station to ask people to call in when they witnessed black ice or accidents. That way we could broadcast the recordings over the airwaves. They loved the idea and decided to go with it. We even had each participating station equipped with the new cellular bag phones, which had a reach of up to 25 miles. They allowed them to do remote broadcasts and cellular weather reports, and they could use them for free if they mentioned Cellular One every time they broadcast, which was also my idea.

The media campaign was a huge success and because of this, Cellular One rolled out their national expansion earlier than expected.

Cellular or mobile phones are almost everywhere in the world today!
Image by pasja1000 Pixabay

The most essential principle in marketing is that you know the primary benefit of your product or service. You also need to understand how your targeted audience's needs will be satisfied. Through this principle, the buyers dominated the airwaves with the corporate sponsorship of the "Cellular One Road Reports" on all the main Spokane radio stations!

In college we learned that most advertising dollars are focused on and directed toward women. There is also another group that is very vocal. Its members are great communicators for marketing messages: the youth. The audiences who ignite the media and make it catch fire are those who are eighteen to twenty-four years old, along with the next group: women who are twenty-four to forty-five. When you primarily focus on these two groups, they provide the best impetus for media success.

Make Yourself Stand Out

WHAT IS YOUR DIFFERENTIATION? (REASON)

One of the most exciting grand opening campaigns was for a brand-new car dealership in North Idaho. They had five separate new car franchises: Subaru, Nissan, Jaguar, Volkswagen, and Audi. They had decided to make a huge splash and promote their event heavily. As the radio rep, I had gone over the night before to make sure it was a go for Saturday's grand opening. I had the responsibility for coordinating the remote live broadcast. It could make or break the promotion. Let me explain.

Midway Imports had purchased quite a few items to give away so they could generate in-store traffic. For example, they gave away an expensive generator and other lavish gifts that were not cheap.

The dealership did not spare any expense. They had made a solid radio buy, especially since it was early November and Christmas was still far away.

The owner of Midway had wanted the live remote broadcast to start at 9 a.m. the next day, which I thought was a little early. My fellow DJ and I traveled the following day, after the storm had dumped 8 inches of fresh powder. It was our first snowstorm of the season. Getting over there was tricky because it was a 30-mile drive east of Spokane on I-90, and it was located in the beautiful resort town of Coeur d'Alene, Idaho.

For the remote broadcast, we planned to catch people early Saturday morning before they left home, especially those who worked a regular workweek. Even with this preparation, it was scary in the first two hours because the live remote was relatively uneventful. We only saw a handful of people. Yikes!

The dealer principal came over to me and asked if we could cancel or reschedule the rest of the broadcast until sometime later because people were simply not coming in. The snow was beginning to melt, and it was beautiful since the sun had just come out. However, because there had been so much snowfall, it was still very tough traveling.

That's when a light bulb went on in my head. I said, "Wait a minute! How many different all-wheel drive and four-wheel drive vehicles do you have to choose from?"

He became enthusiastic and excited, boasting, with his chest sticking out.

"We have more four-wheel-drive and all-wheel-drive vehicles to pick from than any other dealer in the entire Inland Northwest," he said.

I responded, "Wow! That's great news, and we need to tell our listeners!"

Knowing your critical difference from your competition is what I call differentiation. It is a principle I believe makes all the difference.

There was quite a turnaround when we blasted the message out to the masses. In thirty minutes, we saw a steady stream of people come in. Actually, it was more than a stream. It was a flood of people, and they were not kicking tires. They were sitting down to buy new vehicles.

Now, please understand that as far as competition went, Seattle is more than 300 miles to the west. Lots of car buyers traveled there for what they believed were better deals. The trade area here was approximately 150 miles in any direction, including Canada, as the border was only a couple of hours north.

The timing couldn't have been better. When the dealer mentioned to me that he wanted to pull the plug, I thought the car shoppers were not coming out because of one reason, the snow. Granted, it was early on in my career, and I was just getting my feet wet. This type of learning was way better than the textbooks at the university.

When we left an hour later, four or five couples were lined up at each closing booth. The salespeople were not test-driving but sitting down and taking orders. The results seemed to have been practically instantaneous after we started telling everyone on the radio that this was the time to buy a four-wheel-drive vehicle. The urgency was paramount, and if they could get in, there was no better time to buy than now!

The steps to marketing effectiveness are to uncover the need, broadcast your difference, dominate the marketing, and develop momentum.

The following Monday at our 9 a.m. sales meeting at the radio station, a manager from the dealership rushed in to say he needed to talk to me. After our receptionist escorted him to our conference room, he stuck out his hand and in front of everyone said, "I want to thank you for what you did for us over the weekend because we sold over seventy cars for the dealership, and I sold seventeen cars myself!"

It was an offer that had capitalized on urgency; the need was amplified, creating an incredible reaction. The most basic and fundamental change made all the difference. The timing was perfect, and it made for a very memorable grand opening. The key was coming up with a solution together and knowing the right question to ask about what makes your business stand out from all your competition.

PROMOTE YOUR GREATEST STRENGTH (DOMINANCE)

One of my largest clients in the yellow pages was an attorney in Arizona. I found him by calling businesses listed in the phone book's white pages who were not advertisers. At the time, I was training our sales reps and showing them how to make phone calls to prospective clients, in what was called "dialing for dollars." Right out of the gate, we asked them a simple question, which opened up the conversation and created an immediate dialogue with the potential client.

DELIVER
BOLDNESS!

We had twenty publications in the outlying areas of Arizona but nothing in the actual Phoenix metro market. I taught the new sales reps to lead with this question: "What are you doing to market yourself in the areas outside of the Phoenix metro market?" This was our highest point of differentiation because all of the other eight different phone books were going for the ad dollars of the metro market. We were going after the local neighborhood dollars!

Through asking this question, we told them our key difference right out of the gate. Then, we would open up the conversation and create a dialogue on the phone with the potential client.

One day, I was practicing "cold calling" with Robert. I hated to use that term because through this technique you can uncover many hidden gems. Anyway, I ended up speaking with an attorney named Adam. He responded to my question with, "Whatcha got?" He was very interested in talking and wanted to meet ASAP, and he asked the price for a full-page ad in color in all of our publications state-wide (with all of them paid in full). This was quite a surprise, and Robert loved this lesson of "dialing for dollars!" Get this—no one had contacted him from our media firm for the last three years.

When we went to see Adam, Robert and I met him at his office, which was in his home on the fairway of a Scottsdale golf course. When we entered his office, we surprisingly found it to be in his luxurious living room, which overlooked the beautiful course.

He stated that he had no secretary, and this certainly grabbed our attention. I asked him if he would mind sharing his unique method of doing business and the reasons for his successful growth. He then explained his unorthodox business setup and personal style.

Adam said that he spent over $200,000 a year[21] on advertising and had been doing this for more than ten years. His return was an average of 2,000 phone calls a year, and he would pick the top thirty accident cases to be his clients. It was an incredible business model that produced multi-million-dollar returns on investment. (I should point out that this was in 2007.)

It was evident that I was dealing with a seasoned professional, and after negotiating a solid deal for

---

[21] Adjusted for inflation, $200,000 in 2007 was equal to $276,315 in 2022.

him to have twenty full-page color ads in all of our publications, I noticed something about his ad that stood out to me. He had his name and color picture in the ad, but he also included a prominent banner across the top in bold red color that asked, "SERIOUS INJURY?" When I asked him how the ad had worked for him, he said, "It works great!"

In this case, I didn't offer any other suggestions, and we began to discuss other marketing ideas involving the web and Google. Surprisingly, he wasn't the least bit interested. He had achieved a phenomenal marketing response by positioning himself dominantly with massive exposure. Adam was dead serious in his approach to marketing and advertising. This showed me that he had achieved massive momentum with an abundance of clients.

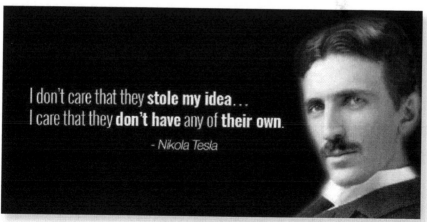

My six most powerful words were, 'I have an idea for you!'
Image by Goalcast

MAKE IT FUN AND SIMPLE (CREATIVE SELLS)

One of my clients had a pet store named Pets Are People Too, which was located in Moscow, Idaho. The store served two towns with universities, the University of Idaho and also Washington State, which is 8 miles west, in Pullman, Washington.

They were preparing for a holiday advertising blitz between Thanksgiving and Christmas and wanted something that would help promote their holiday business. They had also tried broadcast radio in the past but said it didn't work. That was a challenge for me because it inspired me to go deeper and discover what makes marketing and advertising work. In my mind, this holiday blitz needed to be both unusual and creative in its approach. The one thing I wanted to bring home to people's minds was the name of the business: Pets Are People Too.

When I went back to the radio station and started collaborating with Jay, our production manager, I had something in mind. I wasn't sure whether we could pull it off, but I thought it would be fun to try.

After I mentioned I had another challenging demo spot, Jay asked me, "What is it?"

I said, "Growing up as a kid, I used to listen to this album over and over, and it was by Alvin and the Chipmunks. Do you think there is any way I can sing a song and make it sound like them?"

He asked me if I had the words that I wanted to use and asked, "What are they?"

I sang these words: "What are you giving your pet this year? Pets Are People Too-oo-oo! Maybe a bird-house, a dog cage, a rug, or maybe a 10-gallon aquarium. Or maybe you just want a pet—to have and to hold and to keep in your bed. Pets Are People Too-oo-oo, and that is the truth-uth-uth!"

He said, "I love it!"

After coaching me on how to record the lyrics and get the same effect as the Chipmunks, I had a demo spot ready in short order. This guy was such a production genius, and he said I had to be the one to do the commercial because he wasn't going to touch it with a 10-foot pole! I had gone to speak with the client after the holiday, and she had mentioned that people were coming in talking about the commercial.

When I asked her, "What are they saying?" she replied, "Well, several said they had heard it at work on the radio. One said that when the commercial came on and they heard the Chipmunks singing, everyone in the office came over to the radio to listen because it got their attention."

A couple of years ago, I went back and visited the station owner Susan, and told her about my efforts to write this book on marketing.

She said, "You know people still talk about that commercial from thirty years ago?"

I asked, "Which one? 'Another One Rides the Bus'?"

She said, "Yeah, that one too, but the one where you sang 'Pets Are People Too!'"

I said, "Oh, really, still after all these years?"

"Yes, it was great, even after all these years!" she said emphatically.

That commercial branded the name "Pets Are People Too" in pet owners' minds. The momentum that was created lasted well beyond that holiday season. Thirty years later, local people were still talking about it! Susan Weed[22] said they were able

---

[22] https://www.linkedin.com/in/susan-weed-a87b9514/

to add a second location after that because the business had grown so successfully.

> *There is a certain logic to events that*
> *pushes you along a certain path. You go*
> *along the path that feels the most true,*
> *and most according to the principles that*
> *are guiding you, and that's the way*
> *the decisions are made.*
> *—Michael Nesmith*

GREAT OFFERS GET RESULTS (PROMOTE THE LOSS LEADER)

The longest promotion I ever did with a radio station was an entire summer event with a bowling alley. As you may know, bowling alleys have a hard time getting people to come in during the summer, especially on Friday nights. We were looking for an event that promoted good, clean fun for our listeners. Also, selling some air time to an advertiser who normally wouldn't spend any money seemed to me like a good idea.

We already had a good Saturday event with the Christian radio station I was working with. We were giving away free passes to a popular water park throughout the summer, so when I went in to talk to the owner of the local bowling alley, I asked him if Friday night would work. He assured me it would be a great night to promote. My suggestion was that if we could make a strong offer, I knew we would pack the place. With the bowling alley filled, they would make a lot of money through food and beverage sales. He agreed and said he would be willing to cut the cost to "$1 a game with a free shoe rental" every Friday night for the entire summer. This was clearly a great loss leader, and boy, were we going to promote it. We started promoting the event that we called the "Friday Night Super Bowl," located at the Holiday Bowling Alley. We were surprised that having the promotion for the entire summer produced such a great response. The first week just a few people (about 75) came in. It was far from packed, but I saw that the campaign had potential.

–GREAT offers GET Results

With this awareness, we asked those who came in to begin inviting their friends and family. Besides, who doesn't want to take someone to the Super Bowl? "Each One—Bring One!" was the message we kept repeating. It seemed to have quite an effect—not only on participation but also on building the Body of Christ. When new people came in, we invited them to speak with us. We would introduce them on the air and ask the newcomers where they were from and what brought them in. Hearing their responses drew even more people! Since we were broadcasting live updates throughout the night, lots of new attendees spoke on the air.

People who were driving around town or listening at home heard the broadcast and responded by coming in. The campaign created a snowball effect because of the fear of missing out (F.O.M.O.) factor. The most effective local campaigns, in my experience, have been word of mouth with twelve- to eighteen-year-olds.

Each week after that, it continued to build. In three weeks, we packed the place, and the owner couldn't believe how successful the promotion had become. Although it was normally a dead time for them, the Super Bowl had become their best summer event ever. Of course, my kids enjoyed the time, and they felt like celebrities since I would interview them and have them help promote our family fun event. What I learned with this promotion was that when you have a great offer and get people to share it, you will have excellent results.

REAL ESTATE MOMENTUM

One of the most exciting clients I ever worked with was a small family real estate company that bought distressed homes. However, they didn't just flip homes; they rented them out, which I thought was a brilliant idea. After twenty-five years, We Buy Homes of Tucson had amassed several hundred rentals and a sizable net worth.

When I first met Mike, he invited me to consult with him because he had some objectives he wanted to achieve. Before we got into his goals, he gave me a tour of his gorgeous home, which sat directly at the foot of the Tucson Mountains. After showing me his new living room remodel, which he said cost $900,000, I was quite impressed. However, I had no idea of any of this when I first called him to schedule our appointment.

My research before this consultation was fasci-nating. Their foremost competitor was a franchise called HomeVestors. They had an article in the local newspaper published the week before. It was a gold mine of information, detailing the franchise business and even the revenue and cost figures. This information made for a meaningful conversation with my prospective client.

Instead of bringing up his competitor right out of the gate, I asked him what he had done to make himself and his real estate business so successful. I wanted to know about his marketing/advertising positioning in light of their differentiation.

I already knew what Mike was doing in almost all his media. He had been consistently running a 1-inch box display ad in multiple places every day in the local newspaper for the last twenty-five years. In addition to this, he had a yellow page ad in the main phone book and the DEX Phone Book.

When I asked him whether he was excited about his quarter-page yellow page ad in red and white in the real estate category, he said, "No, not at all."

I immediately said, "Neither am I. You should save your money," and I meant it.

I then asked him about his competitors so I could dig down deeper and see how, and if, he wanted to take his business to the next level. My main points of discussion were what he thought of his competitor HomeVestors, and what they were doing for marketing and advertising, and really how much he wanted to compete. Although at that time he wouldn't tell me, I believed his competitor was outspending him about ten to one. I did inform him that they were not my client, and I had read the article in the newspaper the previous week. I knew from the article they were the We Buy Ugly Homes franchise of Southern Arizona and were dividing up the leads among three different franchise owners located in the Tucson Metro area. However, Mike had not seen the article.

When we discussed this, I only asked leading questions and let Mike do the talking. This is one of the great keys to how I was able to take my sales and marketing career to a whole new level. *Listen, after you ask the right question.*

Anyway, Mike thought his competitors probably spent a lot of money on all types of media and had a dominant position in all of them.

We walked into his office, which was located in his palace of a home. I noticed that he had an entire wall of bookcases filled with nothing but phone books. This grabbed my attention, and the light bulb went on in my head and framed the idea for his next opportunity. Mike was dead serious about targeting baby boomers and seniors. This gave me an idea of how we could take his business to the next level.

HomeVestors invested heavily in billboards on the freeways in Tucson. These freeways are on the outside western and southern edges of the city. The traffic was always a mess. It was challenging to navigate across town.

When I asked him what he thought just one billboard cost for a month, he said, "I don't know!" Well, it was my job to know, but I didn't tell him what I knew right then.

I said, "OK, let's talk about this later."

The goal of our meeting was to understand his competitive advantages, his opportunities for his business, and his desire for growth. If there is one thing I have learned in marketing, it's that you are promoting the individuals in the business by tapping into the passions and uniqueness of the individuals who make up their livelihood. It is what I call "the personalization of a business." This is an important factor in working with clients; make it personal.

The takeaway: embrace your clients' goals, desires, and ambitions as your own.

Mike's three primary goals for his business were to hire a good bookkeeper so his wife could enjoy life again, get his office out of his home, and open a new one as a sales center. This improvement would serve well for his son and new manager, Zak, to have a business that would thrive well into the future. After discussing his ambitions and desires for his company, I asked him another billboard question—not how much did the billboard cost, but this: "So Mike, when people are driving 70 miles per hour on the freeway, and they see a 'We Buy Ugly Homes' billboard, what is that phone number?"

He said, "I don't know."

This is when we discussed the idea of putting his main message on the front covers of both of the dominant phone books. Mike told me that people usually called three home-buyer firms for estimates so they could sell their homes quickly. With both leading directories, we had hundreds of thousands of eyes on his message every day throughout the Tucson metro area.

We were capitalizing on their most formidable competitor's advertising, solidly securing the chance of being one of the three phone calls people made when they wanted to sell their distressed homes.

The message we crafted was his main point of differentiation: his slogan, "48 Hours—Fast CASH!" That was the most dominant hot button for his clients, who were satisfied by Mike's great customer service. Having the coveted position on the front cover on the phone book was an expensive proposition, but the next year his business achieved all of his goals and aspirations. As I said before, his son Zak paid me one of the highest compliments I have ever received on LinkedIn: *"Paul Neustrom, you are a marketing genius!"*

When someone has the desire to take their business or career to the next level, the sky's the limit—as long as they are willing to do what is necessary to dominate. In these digital days of "Killing It,"ruling by domination is the most desired achievement for the vast majority of business owners and entrepreneurs.

Take action on your inspirations, and incredible things happen, like I did in the next story.

AUTOMOTIVE MOMENTUM

In honor of me being the top rep in the nation for AutoMart.com, the company flew me out for a sales blitz to Jacksonville, Florida, for an entire week. In fact, all the top-performing reps across the country were there, even the ones I had chased down and passed by using several strategies in this book.

One of the problems I saw other reps struggling with was the retention of clients and dealer principals who had tried our service for three to six months. There were so many similar services available to them, such as Cars.com and our sister company, AutoTrader.com. In their minds, we were "a dime a dozen." But my perspective was a little different. The main reason my clients hired me was not just the service I sold but also everything I brought to the table. My success was in helping boost my dealer's bottom line by becoming actively involved and by teaching them how to effectively use the leads I was delivering.

My very first sales call was to what we called a pot-lot dealer. He had cheap cars and served those needing in-store financing. I will never forget the call for as long as I live because he was a very rude dealer who wanted to make a big impression. Boy, did he ever!

When I introduced myself as Paul Neustrom with AutoMart.com, he retorted, "Who the hell is AutoMart?"

I responded very boldly and confidently with, "Have you ever heard of Google?"

He replied, "Of course I have."

He emphatically stated that he would not support another advertising service for car dealers since there were so many. Then he went further, threatening to call all his car buddies to make sure that none of them would do business with me. He tried to convince me that I would not succeed in my new venture.

Now, there was a lot on the line with this new position. Until then, AutoMart had only been a print publication in convenience stores and had just launched their new internet division. All his threats did was royally hack me off because I knew we were absolutely "Killing It with Google"!

When AutoMart decided to go digital and take their business to the next level, they made some very vital decisions that involved Google. The revamp reminded me of when I launched my internet company, CAReport, ten years prior.

Since we had a ten-year non-compete clause with AutoTrader, we could not launch anything electronically until the mid-2000s. Because of this, when we designed the website, the designers asked Google to be in the room so they could tell us how to dominate their organic listings in search results. This information was essential to my knowledge of how we were different and how we were so dominant online.

When the pot-lot owner said he was going to do everything to defeat me, I knew it was game on—and that the company had made a big decision in hiring me several weeks earlier.

Let me explain. My manager Crystal flew out and offered me the position on the first interview, telling me that they wanted to try an experiment. Typically, they would hire a manager and open an office and pay four sales representatives to hit the streets and sell their services, as they did in Phoenix. However, Tucson was going to be the test market for the rest of the country, and I was the guinea pig!

They wanted me to work out of my own home and drive leads for this new market. My goal was to do it as well as, or better than, other markets. Crystal, the national sales manager, had seen how I had developed the Pacific Northwest territory for an auto rental company into the nation's #1 market, out of fourteen different regions. She thought the gamble would be worthwhile because I had proven myself to be responsible and self-directed while I worked from my home office selling franchises for U-Save Auto Rental.

Offer substance
that resonates & has meaning

Tucson had fewer than a million people and was classified as a small market, what is referred to as a C-Market. This market paled in comparison to Phoenix, which had a population of almost four million. This was a challenge for which I definitely had my work cut out.

My response to Mr. Pot-Lot Dealer was, "OK sir, it's game on!" One thing was clear to me at this moment in my mind: if I am not working for you, then I am working against you. It surprised me how competitive I was at that time. I realized that the leads I generated were for my client dealers. Now, I understand that I work for my clients instead of disagreeable people with negative attitudes. This is a compelling thought and a perspective that is crucial for a salesperson to understand and believe. Our niche was with Google, and we specialized in taking auto dealers, who are the second-most-researched category on the internet, from the traditional (1.0) level to the new (2.0) online platform.

My inspiration and passion is helping business owners take their businesses to a whole new level, creating "NeuStreams of Revenue."

After this realization, I continued the conversation. "So, if you don't mind, I will come in every month and tell you how well my dealers are doing."

Have you ever done something to just prove somebody wrong? The look he gave me was priceless. This,
however, was a defining moment in my career and
the incentive gave me momentum.

I had no idea that presenting a list of results
printed on a four-color postcard would have such
a great impact. It was a dynamic way of promoting
results to dealers. The outcomes of the Google leads
spoke for themselves. We were directing an average
of 160 car buyers to each and every dealer every
month for an average cost of $7.00 per lead. That
was for a phone call or direct inquiry, not just clicks.
Through our new online platform, we made it known
to the whole Tucson automotive community who the
top dealers were. I was providing my dealer clients
with a massive number of potential buyers.

After this formidable confrontation, I decided that
I would only go after the premier car dealers. My
prospect list only included elite dealers, and my sales
vaulted me to become the #1 internet sales rep in
the nation in just six months' time. The Tucson test
market broke all previous sales records and was considered a huge success. This was due in large part to
my previous experience in 1995 with my brand-new
internet company, CAReport. I learned that developing qualified leads and instructing the dealers what

to do with them provided important benefits to my member dealers.

We found with the launch of the CAReport that 70 percent of people were going online to look for high-end cars, such as Audis, BMWs, and Mercedes. They wanted to find the invoice prices so they could go into dealerships with that knowledge and negotiate. However, most dealerships were not willing to go below their minimum profit margins.

Dominate the Market!

One of my greatest strengths is getting the attention of decision makers so I can motivate them to take decisive action right on the spot. In the mid-2000s, dealers were starting to get online in greater numbers. However, there was one dealer in Jacksonville, where I began this story, who was not giving me the time of day. His gatekeeper didn't want the owner to be bothered, so I decided to go for broke. It was in this exchange when I learned that one of my most powerful weapons was the art of creating curiosity with the element of surprise.

Walking in with a business card would have had me striking out at the plate before I even had a chance to swing the bat. (Yes, I used to coach baseball and loved it.) Seeing that I was not getting anywhere with the gatekeeper, I went to plan B. I boldly introduced myself. "Hi! I'm Paul, and I am not sure whether I can help you or not, but if I could ask you one question, would you sit down with me?"

He responded, "Who are you with?"

I ignored him and said, "It's just one question!"

Then he said, "OK, go ahead and ask."

Here was the question: "Of all the business decision you are going to make this year, what is the single greatest decision you could make to take your entire business to the next level?"

He said, "What kind of a question is that?"

I said, "I think it is a pretty good one!"

Then he asked, "What are you selling ... advertising?"

I answered, "Does it matter?" I asked him again, "Of all of the business decisions you will make this year, which one will take you to an entirely different level?" I knew where I wanted to take him with this question. The dealer then said, "OK, sit down!"

On this Jacksonville sales call, the owner did decide to take his business to the next level, and it had a tremendous impact. That week, I was the top-selling rep on the sales blitz because I had learned to ask the right questions. This is the key!

Knowing the powers of Google and understanding its ability to connect shoppers directly to inventory, effectively transformed our auto dealers' bottom lines. It was the most critical decision they could make for their businesses. Therefore, my advice for the #1 thing you can do for your business this year is to get online, develop momentum, and dominate your position.

Remember, catching the wave is an experience of harnessing momentum.

MOST MEANINGFUL MOMENT

The greatest thing about experience is you get the privilege of seeing your ideas produce income year after year for your good clients. I took some of the principles I've mentioned in this book and implemented them with my brother, Patrik. He has been a successful trial attorney and specializes in personal injury and wrongful death cases in Central and Western Kansas. We met up again a short time ago, right before this book was published. We reminisced about some of the ideas we put into place for his practice that he's benefited from for over 15 years. He recounted that they made a difference.

Back in 2005, Patrik had taken most of the firm's traditional marketing and advertising dollars and put them into digital. He wanted to grow his practice more and found the competition online was fierce.

I had seen how you can have great success using traditional marketing and advertising venues to drive leads to digital.

My recommendation to my brother was for him to have a strong digital presence, but not at $60 a click for paid ads on Google. In addition to this, I advised him to keep the messaging consistent across all media. We dominated in such a way that Neustrom and Associates became the go-to law firm for serious personal injury in the state of Kansas.

Patrik took my advice and ran with everything full strength, getting billboards and establishing a strong presence on talk radio. The main piece of advice he has taken for the last fifteen years was to invest in the cover of the phone book—yes, up until 2022. Now you might wonder, why the phone book? As Patrik tells people who question him about it, "I still have clients who contact me from it."

This was a major investment decision for him back in 2006, and the next year he offered to fly me out to consult with him again, although I think he mainly wanted to take me to the Big 12 basketball championships at Kansas University. It was a great game to remember. University of Texas star player Kevin Durant had scored twenty-five points by half-time, helping to give the team its 25-point lead.

It just so happened that the parent company of Lawyers.com and Attorneys.com had heard about my past success as the top digital rep in the nation for AutoMart.com. They wanted to interview me.

The only time we could align our schedules was right at halftime of the KU-Texas basketball game. I had to call the recruiters from inside the very loud Allen fieldhouse because the guard would not allow me to step outside. They asked me where I was because of the noise and suggested I call them back after the game.

Later, I called the recruiters back when I was in the car with my brother. The KU Jayhawks had come back and shut Kevin Durant down in the second half, letting Kansas win sole position of first place in the Big 12.

As the recruiters were asking me their first question, they must have sensed the excitement in the car, and they soon learned how KU had won with a huge turnaround in the second half. In short, Martindale-Hubble wanted me to do the same thing by flying into under-performing markets across the nation to generate a huge turnaround.

One thing I've learned from such interviews is that to give yourself time to think, you can repeat the question back to the questioner. When I responded, "OK, you want me to give you an example of a time when a client took my advice and really grew his law practice." My brother Patrik grabbed the phone and told them the story of how we took his business to the next level just one year before and realized exponential growth. I could tell the interviewers were impressed, but I was especially moved by it. I don't think I ever felt as good in helping a client grow their business as I did then.

MY BROTHER'S SIDE OF THE STORY

"You were there for me and pushed me to assert my experience and skills. You were a catalyst as well as a sounding board for the myriad of ideas I presented. I went solo in 2005 and doubled my ad budget. Our business had not gone down, but we were losing clients to Wichita TV lawyers. People would tell me they did not know I did that kind of work. You told me half of the people assume somebody doesn't do something if it's not listed. So, on our website we started listing brain injury and motorcycle accidents as among the cases we do, and we got the clients.

We were offered the back cover of the phone book fifteen years ago and we decided it would give us a good presence—like a billboard in every home! So, I took it and kept it that entire time. My golfing buddies would kid me about it, and I offered to autograph their phone books. We dominated our 50-mile area. The book was becoming obsolete, but if my friends were kidding me about it, that told me people still saw it. You helped me build a brand and to decide which ideas from my phone book people and marketing firm would work. We are benefiting from your ideas and drive."—Patrik Neustrom[23]

---

[23] Neustrom & Associates website is: http://neustrom.com

PART III

PRINCIPLES OF OVERFLOWING GROWTH

THERE IS NO better way to see overflow principles from your marketing efforts than to help business owners with their Google. I have found the results with internet marketing to be even more dramatic when you optimize their listings. This causes a *Niagara* of things to happen.

In the first chapter, I tell the story of the lowest point of my career. Once I discovered the incredible power of Google marketing and how publishing one photograph could get a million views, I could see how it could help business owners develop. Numbers really communicate when you are talking about getting five to ten times more growth in traffic.

Me helping people with their online marketing feels ironic because this was the media, and especially Google, that killed my career. How did I survive so long selling the old traditional media in a world now dominated by technology? In my last two to three years working in the yellow pages, the only way I could get people to listen to me was by helping them with their online presence. They especially wanted help with Google! They were hungry to learn how to dramatically improve their online presence and search views on the world's largest search engine.

I ended up setting a record at work by selling twenty-eight new yellow page customers. One of them was the owner of a brand-new steakhouse who bought the back cover on the phone book. In exchange, I created a fully optimized Google listing for her and a "killer website" with a social media presence. She did 2.5 million dollars in sales in her first year. I began to see the power in being a local search pro.

My adventurous self!

That was when I discovered that the power of Google isn't in Google Search, it's in Google Maps. For businesses, this really is Google's backbone. When you search for something on Google Maps and it comes up with the top-three businesses, that's called the Google 3-Pack.

Several years earlier, I really discovered "The Power of Google" with a public utility company in Grangeville, Idaho. They were the only gas and water company in the area. They needed help and asked me if I could change the name of their new website. Since I was working with their yellow pages and handling their listings, they thought maybe I could help them with their Google. They just didn't know how to do it. With my cell phone, I made the change right there on the spot. Something like that used to take a week, but by the time I got to my car in the parking lot, the change was already made. It dawned on me how powerful a tool I had in my smartphone.

When I walked into businesses after that, I imagine they probably saw me as just a yellow page sales guy off the street, but I'd already done this Google thing several hundred times before. The power of a Level 7 Google Local Guide impressed them. The more I did, like changing web addresses or posting pictures, the more power and influence I had with Google.

Business owners always tell me they hate getting phone calls several times a day from people who offer to help them with Google. Most of the time, the callers are overseas. Being local and meeting face-to-face makes all the difference in the world. Now I can offer a lot more to them than I could before. To train others in the power of Google and how they can help other business owners with their new-found Google know-how is why I started Certified Search Pros.

Maybe you can remember or imagine looking in the phone book for a taxi company phone number on page 1 of the white pages, where you would read names like AAA Taxi Cabs, AA Cabs, and ABC Taxis. Those listed under A through E in the directory got 80 percent of all lookups.

People have asked me to tell them the most interesting name of a business I ever helped. There was one that had seventeen A's in its name. It was AAAAAAAAAAAAAAAAAway We Go Travel. Back then, if you didn't have one of the first large display ads in the yellow pages, then you hoped to be seen in the first alphabetical listings in that yellow pages category.

Why do I mention all these details? As a sales trainer, I taught new hires everything they needed to know about the basics. Just like in collegiate athletics, mastering the basics makes all the difference for success—like it will for you.

We could make or break a business with their phone book listings. I was not only helping them to get listed in the telephone directory, I also had the opportunity to sell dominant display advertisements. This is how I learned the power of the top-three businesses in the yellow pages. With Google, it is all about dominating. Now we only have one main database to compete in, and it has become highly competitive.[24]

I had one client who was particularly memorable. A roofing contractor called me up two days before the close of our phone book for the coming year. He was new to the area, so the first question he asked me was, "What's the size of this market, and how many directories do you publish?"

As I said before, we had a large market of about a million people in Tucson. I said that we printed and distributed 325,000 directories and that we were one of the top two yellow page directories in town. He then asked, "Do you have a full page available for roofers, where you can guarantee me a top-three position?"

---

[24] https://www.statista.com/statistics/216573/worldwide-market-share-of-search-engines/

What he was referring to was being one of the first three full-page ads in the roofing contractors category.

We weren't supposed to tell them their positions; they would find out once the book was published. With me stalling somewhat, he persisted, "I will buy a full page from you, if you promise me that I'll be in the top three. I will even pay you full rate in color for it, but you have to guarantee it."

I went to my sales manager and asked, "Can I guarantee a full page in color in the top three for a new roofer in town?"

He said, "No, we don't do that."

I continued, "He's willing to pay full rate if we do it, and we only have a couple days before we close the book."

Sometimes the real job of selling is on the sales manager. Michael, my manager, whispered, "OK, we'll do it."

I met with the roofing contractor and signed him up at full rate for a full page and both of us were excited!

Three months after the book had hit the streets, I went to see him and asked, "How is the full-page ad working?"

He responded, "It's great! It always works great. Every market I've ever been to, if I'm in the top three in roofing with a full-page ad, I always dominate. I'm a roofing broker, so what I do is I get the jobs from the homeowners, and then I go out and hire other roofers to do the work."

This business owner was killing it with yellow pages way before Google was around. What this taught me was that to win, you have to fully commit yourself to the cause and not just go through the motions. This applies to all of us. Either "Go big or stay home!" Today, with your online marketing, like in the yellow pages, you want to be in the top three on Google. The next few stories are examples of how *prevailing online* helped businesses really thrive.

GOING FROM EMPTY TO FILLED— AIRBORN DISC GOLF PRESERVE

In the previous section on momentum, we looked at a collection of stories about success that was beyond the average. The businesses had over-the-top out-comes that far exceeded people's expectations. Stories give unique perspectives to convey under-standing in a way that goes beyond just books of theory. The stories show what the problems were, how we went about solving them, and finally, what we learned from them while measuring the results. The next story is an example of this.

Several months ago, I moved to a location on the Mississippi River. Near our place is an old, abandoned golf course that had gone bankrupt. Last fall, when we started to take walks, we would head along the old course. Soon, a group of young people decided to start a disc golf course. They converted the two nine-hole courses into several of the top-renowned disc golf courses in the nation. They even hosted nationals there last year.

COMPETITION & MARKET CONDITION

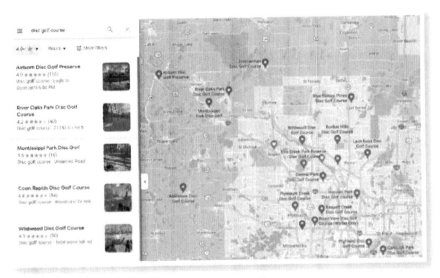

Search results for disc golf courses

This spring, they reopened the course for the coming season and found that their Google Maps listing had been permanently closed. Since I'm a Google reviewer, I offered to help them. When I checked the back end of the listing on Google Maps, I saw that it was, in fact, permanently closed. I could not even open it. Because of this, I had to be inventive and try a few different things.

First, I submitted a brand-new listing to Google, changing the business name to the current one, Airborn Disc Golf Preserve, and putting "Now Open" in parentheses. After doing this, and getting the listing opened back up, in a period of about three months, their listing had over 40,000 views. In the back end of their listing, I could see that their search views went up 450 percent, and their Google Maps views went up 150 percent.

When I began to see results for clients in numbers like these, I felt I had something of worth to offer people. All of my years as a yellow page salesman were paying off, and I began to have a sense of fulfillment.

The key is to learn how to master the basics.

With this particular optimization, I found that the actual clubhouse and tavern were interested in having me help them further. Because of this, we posted some photographs and did an actual event where we had some entertainment come in. The turnout was more than expected. This shows how they jumped up to the #1 rank quickly.

Competitor Comparison		
Business	Rating	Reviews
AirBorn Disc Golf Preserve	4.9	110
River Oaks Park Disc Golf	4.2	40
Montissippii Park Disc Golf	4.8	16

They immediately got traction because there was traffic searching for them. I posted the best picture from their website, and it got 5,000 views in the first week. I use this as an example of an existing business that has already gone from lost to found, but in this case, they went from empty to partially filled. It's not enough to be partially filled; you want to be completely filled.

GOING FROM PART-FILLED TO FULL

One day my girlfriend and I were at a gas station, getting fuel after running some errands.

From the wall of Selena's Salon

I saw a little sign that said "U.S. Nails." It had an arrow pointing toward a strip mall about half a block away. I could see that they were trying to get business but, being off the main road, they were struggling to do so.

Being curious, I scheduled an appointment. I met Selena, the owner who was doing a really great job of taking care of her customers. I could see this from her online reviews. Both my girlfriend and I liked her. She had good reviews, and from them and my own personal observation, I could tell she was a really sweet person. They had been open for a while and had a small customer base, but I could see that Google could take them from just making it to doing well. The key was if we could get U.S. Nails into Google's top three.

I asked Selena, "Would you like some help with your Google listing?"

She responded, "Sure!"

I offered to help her out in exchange for services. I worked with Selena and optimized her online listing and created a fully optimized website with Google, as well as with Apple Maps. However, the main thing I wanted to do for her was not just bring her up in the search results but also raise her to the top of the organic listings.

COMPETITION & MARKET CONDITION

Competitor Comparison		
Business	**Rating**	**Reviews**
U. S. Nails and Nail Salon	4.8	40
Super Nails	4.5	61
Sara Nails	4.5	54

When you search "nail salons" in this city, you will find seventy different stores listed. Because of this, I invested some time and effort in search engine optimization. The results were respectable in the first three months, Selena's listings and views went from 1,100 to 6,600 a month. In the following two months, her views and searches went up to 8,800.

Needless to say, Selena was ecstatic. She's had to bring her sister on as a full-time employee to handle the extra business. Sometimes when I'm visiting, her phone will ring ten times in just a few minutes. As a business growth coach, this is music to my ears! Selena gets the best reviews, and her responsiveness to her customers is what makes all the difference.

Research suggests that every negative review you get that you fail to handle properly can cost you as many as 30 new customer opportunities.
—David Wanamaker[25]

SECRET OF REVIEWS

The secret of reviews is a bigger deal than you would imagine. If you own a business, no matter what your industry or interest, your reviews are your bread and butter for attracting new clientele. This is a big reason for U.S. Nails' rise to the #1 ranking. Optimizing their

---

[25] David Wanamaker - Owner - Five Star Solutions Group
https://www.linkedin.com/in/david-wanamaker-66a4044/

Google listing was also a necessary catapult for their business. Selena really didn't have time to do this, so having a local search pro made all the difference for her business.

This is a search for local nail salons. Selena is the #1 U.S. Nails & Nail Salon. I added the two keywords of *nails* and *nail salon* together because it gives her a unique advantage to be listed as both.

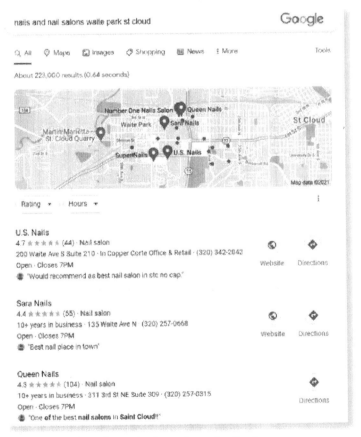

Search results for nails and nail salons

The primary reason that businesses don't effectively manage their reviews is that they don't know what to do or how to do it. Most owners are far too busy to keep tabs on all of the various review sites. Even if they could, they wouldn't check them frequently enough to take appropriate action. SecretofReviews.com is an automated system we had developed for our customers who want to monitor and manage their reviews but don't have the time to do it themselves. With The Secret of Reviews, you can monitor review sites and it will alert you via email when a review is left about your business. It's like putting your reviews on autopilot.

Most businesses do good work and provide great services, but the problem is that most happy customers don't go out of their way to post about good experiences online. As a consequence, your prospects only hear from the customers who have had negative experiences.

The best defense to turn this around is simply a great offense. Stop negative ads before they happen. In our system, we teach a simple review process, and it filters people who report unfavorable experiences so that the business owner can handle them before they are given an opportunity to publish a negative online review.

This is a great tool to help you gain valuable feedback from customers and resolve issues that are impacting them, so you can turn your positive reviews into noticeably more business.

As shown in this story, by building and capturing momentum, you can dominate with the #1 position on Google if you learn the secrets and take effective action. As I said earlier, The Secret of Reviews is a bigger deal than you have imagined. If you own a business, or if you want to help business owners and entrepreneurs with their marketing, your reviews are the holy grail for attracting new customers and clients. Reviews are the word-of-mouth advertising of today.

Today, Google is the go-to arena for the race to win in online marketing. It has pushed the competition to heights never seen before. In these digital days, "Killing It with Google" is the most desired achievement for local business owners and entrepreneurs. The question is, how do you learn to compete in such a ruthless and cutthroat world? Remember, one of the most important considerations is the staggering number of people who are searching for businesses every second of every day on Google, Instagram, and Facebook.

Want to know more? Click here to learn more about SecretofReviews.com.

FILLED TO OVERFLOWING—AIRBORN DISC GOLF PRESERVE

Photo courtesy of airbornpreserve.com

This was the second season for the new disc golf course in our area, and it was a dramatic year in terms of the numbers attracted. The year before had been the opening year of the course, as you read earlier. They had done a great job establishing their presence with two courses that were both already recognized as top-rated. They caught a lot of attention.

One thing that is true about marketing is that you don't create traffic, you capture it.

Airborn Preserve Disc Golf ⌄
1100 Main St, Clearwater, MN 55320, United Stat...

Views	Searches	Activity
13K	7.6K	6.4K

Website visits	74	+9 (14%)
Calls	32	+25 (357%)
Photo views	6.3K	+809 (15%)
Direction requests	38	+16 (73%)

Performance over the past 28 days

Earlier, I mentioned that their Google listing had been permanently closed and it was a challenge to get it opened. After we did, at the start of the 2021 season in April, we saw the numbers increase from 692 searches and 1,100 views by over 10 times and 18 times, respectively, by the end of July. *The activity* level increased by an incredible number.

We knew the numbers for the Preserve Championship, the seventh stop on the 2021 Disc Golf Pro Tour, were going to be huge. When we drove by the event, the parking lot was ridiculously crowded. It was so packed that a grandmother of a staff member said it reminded her of Woodstock in 1969, the largest music concert in history at the time.

The number of competitors who entered the Preserve Championship had more than doubled from the year before. The mass of spectators went up remarkably, a testament to our capturing the wave of online traffic, especially from Google. This is why I find this to be so exciting—because great things can happen, and we have the numbers to prove it.

Photo courtesy of airbornpreserve.com

Today Google is the bedrock of marketing; the basics we do for businesses build on this foundation to grow from empty to overflowing.

NEUSTREAM MARKETING

Today, Google is winning the race in online marketing, and it has pushed the competition to heights never seen before. Everyone knows the most dominant arenas of competition in this market are the triopoly known as Facebook, Google, and Amazon. They control almost two-thirds of

Paul Neustrom, owner of NeuStream Media and KillingItOnline.com

the world's entire ad market and will be pushing up to hundreds of billions in ad revenue in the future. Have you noticed how the term "Google" has mutated from a noun into a verb? For instance, we say "Google it" instead of "search for it." The word has adapted because people find incredibly useful information through Google's search engine. If you think this is an accident or coincidence, then think again.

You see, Google has developed a mutually beneficial system for itself and other businesses throughout the world. Here's why: if Google understands your business, then it can provide accurate information to its users about it. This way Google makes a lot of money from its advertisements and paid services. The first step to going from "lost to found" with online marketing is to get found on all the platforms, with the ultimate goal of being "Filled to Overflowing"!

GOOGLE BUSINESS PROFILES

To store and show accurate information about local businesses, Google has developed a tool originally called Google My Business (GMB). However, they keep changing the name. It is now called Google Business Profiles. Basically, this is our modern-day version of the yellow pages. If you follow some simple steps to upload your business's information to Google, it will give you the equivalent of a free full-page and full-color ad.

Many business owners are already taking advantage of Google Business Profiles. If they aren't, then it is usually because they don't have time for it and need a local search professional to help them.

What percentage of online searches are done on Google?

Handling over 90 percent of all search queries worldwide, Google is undoubtedly dominating the global search engine market share. As of

*June 2021, a whopping 92.6 percent
of all search queries conducted across
all search engine providers are done
through the internet giant.*
—Oberlo.com[26]

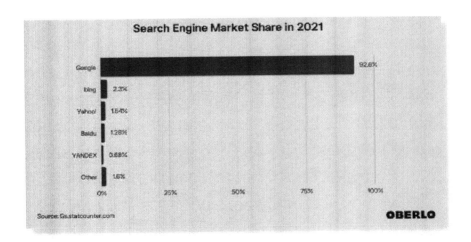

What do you do most of the time? You Google it!
If you have any doubts, think about your own experience researching new companies online. You're more
likely to purchase from the ones with a well-estab-
lished web presence, like on Google, since statistics
show nine out of ten people do the same. Those companies appear more professional and modern, immediately instilling consumer trust. By focusing on your
business's listing on Google, you can easily gain the

---

[26] https://www.oberlo.com/statistics/search-engine-market-share

upper hand on your competition. The way to prevail and win in marketing is to compete with everything you have and not hold back.

Now that you've learned about the importance of being in the top three of Google, here is another benefit that Google provides. If you are a church or a nonprofit, Google has options available to you, and we also have resources that can help you take your marketing to a higher level when you are ready.

If you are a marketing entrepreneur and want to help others in your area to dominate on Google, then this is a great income-generating career for you. Contact us: Certified Search Pros.

GOOGLE'S FREE—$10,000 GRANT FOR NONPROFITS/501(C)3'S

As churches and nonprofits are looking for opportunities to spread their ministries effectively, they may find that capturing website traffic is a good option for them. If this is the case, Google Ad Grants give certain organizations—including churches—the opportunity to use AdWords for free. This can increase organic traffic to their websites when properly done. These grants offer a virtually unlimited budget for churches to finance their website advertising. They can start at $10,000 a month, and it can go up as high as $120,000 a year. And did I say, it is *free*?

To have a successful campaign, the church should not emphasize just its landing page. For example, it should also lead people to other pages that encourage calls to action, such as signing up for the church's email list. This allows the organization to maximize earnings from donations and increase conversion and click-through rates. If the church does well with the Google Ad Grants for six months, they will get access to Google Ad Grants PRO and can receive $40,000 per month. However, if a church is smaller, it may find that a larger grant is unnecessary.

Overall, Google Ad Grants are not the right fit for everyone. However, they can offer resources that benefit certain ministries. Discover the possibilities you may be missing out on by contact us at: NeuStream Media at NeuStreams.com.

FEAR IS OUR GREATEST OPPORTUNITY

Sometimes our trials push us in new directions, and there is nothing worse than feeling like you are stuck, where you lack desire and motivation. As you heard before, I know what it is like to have loved and lost everything. There is an immobilizing fear in not knowing how to start all over again. Did this test my patience and faith? Sure it did. Did I think about just

I was born Terry but had a "Road to Damascus" experience like the Apostle Paul and legally changed my name to Paul Neustrom.

giving up? Yes. The hardest thing to overcome was feeling like I had nothing of worth to contribute. When you are in a state of fear, everything becomes difficult.

*Many times what we perceive as an error
or failure is actually a gift. And eventually we find that lessons learned from
that discouraging experience prove
to be of great worth.*
—Richelle E. Goodrich

Let me tell you about my experience with fear and how I overcame it, because victory from fear can move you from empty to filled to overflowing. The way to overcome fear is to learn to deal with it in an effective way. To get on top of your fears, you have to recognize you cannot defeat them entirely by not thinking about them. You have to enter into your fears and, in effect, embrace them, as you will see in the following stories.

FEARS AND ASPIRATIONS OF THE LOST

Let's dive into the most frightening experience of my existence, which illustrates the importance of the principle of dealing with the real fears I had before.

I was just learning to swim when my older brother Patrik took me up on the high diving board. It seemed higher than anything I had ever jumped from, let alone dove from. There I was, shaking like a leaf and filled with fear. I was only six years old and I couldn't move. This diving stuff was scary! My mind was racing! Would I fall off the edge and hit the pavement of the pool or hit the water so hard I would drown? Or would I chicken out because I was too afraid to try? From that height, the only thing I was seeing was a vision of me busting my head wide open, like I had done the year before, after my sister had warned me not to climb across two large rocks. I did anyway, and the next moment I had a rude awakening. I fell headlong, and I split my head open on a huge pile of rocks. Carole ran down the mountainside, carrying me as blood was streaming down my head. I required a lot of stitches, and it is safe to say I had some good sense knocked into me.

This wouldn't be the last time my two older brothers would challenge me to rise to their expectations. Competitiveness, drive, and ambition ran deep in our family. Because of these values, we had an unspoken duty to always do the absolute best we could do. Our dad was the leader in that department because he was nothing short of a perfectionist. Most of us kids followed right behind him.

My brother was bound and determined to teach me to dive from the high board that day. In his resolve, he knew the only way I was going to overcome my fear was to face it head on and take the plunge. He was forcing me to embrace my fear!

Honestly, I felt like crawling out to the end of the board. I was fearing the worst because I instinctively knew the saying "It is not the fall that kills you but the sudden stop at the end."

Growing frustrated with my refusal to "Just go for it," he came up behind me, grabbed my ankles, and carried me upside down by my ankles as he walked to the end of the board. Then my brother ordered me to "Make like an arrow!" I had no doubt he was going to send me to my probable death in the deep pool below. Now, understand I had learned how to dog paddle only the year before. My mind raced to remember a prayer, but I could utter nothing!

Suddenly, my brother let go of me and I plunged into the perilous depths of the municipal pool below. Then, all of a sudden, an incredible feeling came over me. It was the wildest sensation I had ever felt. It was fun and I wanted to do it again!

HAVE NO FEAR, ONLY BELIEVE!

Thinking back to such foundational moments, it was *almost* like a baptism into living a life free from fear! Who knew that I would go on to compete and win in quite a few gymnastics and diving competitions? I had a goal of going to the 1976 Olympics, so I buckled down to pursue my dream. Yet, as I plunged headlong, it seemed like something was holding me back.

In the beginning of my freshman year, my coach, Jack Harris, had made a profound impact on me. It was a moment that I would carry with me for the rest of my days. Training for my first competition, my coach told me something I will never forget.

I remember back to the first and biggest high school gymnastics meet of the year. The competition was sizable because the 5A and 4A divisions, and the rest of the state, were invited. There was no other time during the year with as big an event as this, not even the State Championships. However, this was my debut as a freshman in my high school career. I had been an exhibitioner the year before as an eighth grader, but my score didn't count. Even then, I had started to catch some notice from some of the judges when my scores were higher than those of the other guys competing.

However, that became a thing of the past when we were warming up for the Wichita East Invitational. I was sitting on the bench, watching a high school senior from Dodge City, Kansas, perform every trick in the book. He was wowing the crowd with what he did, in his bright red tights and long hair. They were applauding him as he successfully completed each warm-up pass.

I sat with my head hung low, thinking, "This guy is really good!"

Some of my teammates had told me that he had just accepted a full-ride scholarship to UCLA. As a freshman in my first competition for a real score, I was feeling defeated in my mind before I even stepped out onto the gymnastics floor.

Coach Harris saw that I was upset. He came over to me and asked, "Son, what's the matter?" Now, the only person who had ever called me Son before was my dad, who was then with my mom in the stands in the front row of the balcony.

I responded, "Coach, that guy can throw every trick in the book. There is no way I can beat him!"

Without any hesitation whatsoever, he said, "Sure you can."

I asked, "Do you really think so?"

Then he said these words that rang true in my soul. "Neustrom, you are much cleaner than he is. All you have to do is hit your routine because, you know, clean wins!"

I challenged him and asked again, "Coach, do you really think so?"

He repeated emphatically, "I know so—just hit your routine and you will win!" I loved him for that quote because it completely changed my course.

If there was one thing I had learned, it was that scoring is mainly about form, like having your toes pointed and legs together as you do your tumbling passes, rather than wowing the crowds with your fantastic tricks.

Success is something that can be self-programmed into you, but it's a matter of being aware of what to do and tapping into it.

This is when my training took over, and all the diving and flips and twists began to settle down in my mind. I began to focus, just as I had done for hours on end before I went to sleep at night. I recalled my workouts where I had to do five clean routines before I could go home from practice.

Needless to say, I was nervous but also excited. Luckily, I got to go first up in the prelims before the dude from Dodge City.

My inner voice was telling me, *Don't be afraid. You can do it. Go for it! You can win!*

Winning anything happens first in the mind. Seeing it in your mind is critical. If you can positively focus on it, you can achieve it.

Well, when my scores came up for the preliminaries, I was tied with the UCLA-bound gymnast with the red tights. We both received 8.95's. It was the first time I had ever received a 9.0 score from a judge, and two of the four judges gave it to me. 10.0, was a perfect score back then., where now it is 15.

That evening, with my parents watching and my coach encouraging me, I focused on the task at hand, concentrating, and not picturing anything but victory.

That day, something happened to me in the final round. I nailed my routine and beat out my senior competitor, receiving a 9.0 final score. It was the most powerful feeling. The real nemesis I had defeated was—*fear!*

It was in this place I discovered the pure outright confidence and inspiration that came from encouragement and intense focus. It was an exhilarating experience, to say the least, one that showed me that when you go for it and have victory from fear, great things will happen.

VICTORY FROM FEAR

Gymnastics is a sport that not only requires a great amount of physical strength, flexibility, balance, coordination, and agility, but also a certain degree of grace. Being free from fear is not a prerequisite for this, but it certainly helps. Oftentimes, those who have a high degree of passion for the sport find a way to overcome their fears.

"Anyone can train to be a gladiator. What marks you out is having the mindset of a champion." Manu

Bennett, the author of this quote,[27] is an actor who portrayed the Gallic gladiator Crixus in the TV series *Spartacus*. Now, gymnastics is not acting, but I know from experience the saying that gymnastics is 95 percent mental is correct.

When I was in high school and had a winning start as a freshman, I struggled to sleep. I would constantly go through my tumbling routines in my mind, almost in slow motion, as I broke down the individual parts. My coach Jack Harris would comment sometimes when I would walk into practice, "Terry, it looks like you didn't get any sleep at all last night." I told him that it was true, because I couldn't stop visualizing the routines in my mind.

Now, Harris was also my springboard diving coach in the summer months because diving was the perfect way to stay in shape in the off-season. During that time, he drilled into me: "Practice does not make perfect; it's perfect practice that makes perfect."

He asked me if I was dreaming about my routines or consciously doing them in my mind.

I responded, "No, I am awake and see them in my mind."

---

[27] https://quotefancy.com/manu-bennett-quotes

He told me, "Keep doing this, because it is per-fect practice!"

Vision gets the dreams started.
Dreaming employs your God-given
imagination to reinforce the vision.
Both are part of something I believe is
absolutely necessary to building the life
of a champion, a winner, a person of high
character who is consistently at the top
of whatever game he or she is in.
—Emmitt Smith

Needless to say, gymnastics became more than just a sport to me. It became my everything! One of the most exciting times was when I made it to the top-rated college gymnastics team in the country. It had been a long road getting there since my start in the fifth grade. I was not prepared for the lessons I would learn from my college coach.

I will never forget the first day of gymnastics prac-tice at the university. Francis Allen, the head coach, sat us five freshmen down and said, "OK guys, we are going to really get down to the basics." Then he asked us his bottom-line question: "What do you think is the definition of meekness?"

All of us looked around at each other and shrugged our shoulders and we said we didn't know.

He continued, "If you are thinking that you know it all, I cannot teach you a thing. But if you humble yourself and actually open yourself to learning, I can teach you things that you've always wanted to know." Coach Allen also said, "Meekness is an attitude, when you say to yourself, 'I don't know s***, but I want to learn.'"

The key, according to Allen, was to empty ourselves out so he could work with us. The first thing he asked us to work on was forward rolls on the tumbling mats. To this day, I remember immediately saying to myself, "Now, I know how to do this. He didn't recruit the Kansas State Tumbling Champion for nothing."

I caught myself and repeated his words of instruction, which in my mind still seemed to be the word "weakness." Then we started working on forward rolls, the most basic of tumbling moves. Coach volunteered me to go first to learn the basics of the forward roll, and man was I surprised. I had always left my hands down on the floor, but now I was supposed to end up with my hands above my head. I realized that I had been doing it wrong all along. If your hands are down, you aren't set up right for the next move, because your hands are supposed to be above your head. Otherwise, you will end up where you have to do a front roll into a front flip, and you aren't set up right to do it. *Man, I thought, I really need to take this learning to heart.*

Yes, it was humiliating, but it was also one of the greatest lessons I have ever learned. Coach Allen instilled within us that the mastery of gymnastics is won in a far more important place than on the gym floor. It is won in the mind. He went on to coach the University of Nebraska's gymnastics team to seven national championships. He helped us make history, which brought a lot of recognition to the school and created a sports dynasty.

One of the greatest things for fulfillment is victory from fear!

University of Nebraska-Lincoln gymastics team

COMING BACK FROM DEFEAT

An incredible life-changing event occurred when I was at Nebraska on the #1 ranked team in the country. We lost one meet that season but won the Big 8 Championships. We defeated Iowa State and Oklahoma, the #2 and #3 teams, respectively. There is only one team that advances to the NCAA Championships per conference, and that year it was us!

When we had celebrated our conference win at the University of Colorado in Boulder, we did something rather impulsive. We partied outside by the pool in polar-cold temperatures in very late March. We were not using our common sense.

Two weeks later, four of us came down with mononucleosis, and we ended up taking fourth place at the Nationals. This was an especially devastating time because I was one of the four and I knew something was wrong. It had been a very hard week, and it took everything I had to just get through it. It was then that I began to feel like I was losing everything.

After our defeat, I went back to the hotel to take a quiet soak in the bathtub. I wanted to think about where my life-path had taken me and where I might possibly go from there. I had accomplished almost everything I had set out to do. Once the water turned lukewarm, I decided to let all the water drain out of the tub so I could sit and continue to think. I would make one of my most powerful decisions ever.

My roommate Larry Gerard was an Olympian, as well as two younger gymnasts, Phil Cahoy and Jim Hartung, who were coming up through the ranks in the Nebraska High School program. They were both very talented and would go on to capture world renown. Back when our University of Nebraska men's gymnastics team went on to claim the National Title in 1979, it would be the start of five consecutive national championships, from 1979 to 1983.

Having this incredible experience in the past year, and seeing what had been accomplished, left me evaluating what really held meaning for me. Looking back, I had won five Kansas High School Championship titles thanks to my first coach, Jack Harris. Two weeks before Nationals, I had been praised by my Nebraska coach, Francis Allen, who said, "Neustrom, you are the most consistent gymnast in the nation." You see, I had scored the same score every time that year, except once when I scored higher. When I competed, Coach Allen said he could always count on me. This was probably one of the greatest compliments I had ever received, but there was still something gnawing at me. While I sat in the tub, waiting to dry, I felt like I was at a crossroads.

After what seemed a long time, I was still sitting in the bathtub, completely bone dry, and a small, still voice asked, "Do you feel how empty this bathtub is without water?" I thought to myself, *Well, yes I do!* Then the revelation continued, "This is how empty you are without *Me!*" Before I got out of that tub, I made a promise to my Lord and Savior: "If this is really you, I will do whatever you set before me. Just tell me what to do, Lord!" That's when I realized, *This must be God speaking!* I learned throughout the next forty years that my desire was not just to be filled with His Holy Spirit, but to be filled to overflowing in all aspects of my being.

Picture taken of Terry Paul in Vermont, 1980

These experiences made an incredible impact on me, and because of what I learned from them, they have shaped me to be the person I am today.

There are two ingredients that have been foundational in my story, and what I learned from these experiences was inspiration and enthusiasm. Inspiration is, in its essence, "in-spirit-action" and is an act of the Holy Spirit. This happens once a person confesses that Jesus Christ is his personal Lord and Savior and believes that God raised Him from the dead. The second is "en-Theo," which means "God energized within!"

FOUR WORDS THAT CHANGED ME FOREVER

I have seen that, as humans, we are in one of four places in our lives. We are either empty, part filled, filled to capacity, or ultimately filled to overflowing. When I was seventeen, a couple of guys came up to me in a taco-tico restaurant and spoke four words that changed me forever.

Me as a teenager

They asked me, "Have you found Jesus?"

I didn't know how to respond because I had gone to church my entire life, but I felt empty inside. They said, "Why don't you come to our fellowship?" It turned out to be called the Solid Rock. During my first visit, I was baptized in the Holy Spirit, and it was so amazing because I was filled with the Holy Spirit, but I didn't fully comprehend it. Having grown up in the Episcopal Church, I had never experienced anything like this before.

That memorable night, I began to see that everything else pales in comparison to it. Sports had its high points, but they didn't last. Work has its successes, but nothing compares to being filled and not thirsting anymore. Over time I realized that the Lord had been encouraging me through my entire journey. I believe this is what gave me hope to keep moving forward. My well would be transformed one more time because of God's faithfulness.

*The Lord will guide you continually,
And satisfy your soul in drought, And
strengthen your bones; You shall be like
a watered garden, And like a spring of
water, whose waters do not fail.*
—Isaiah 58:11–12 (NKJV)[28]

[28] https://www.biblegateway.com/passage/?search=Isaiah%2058:11-12&version=NKJV

I will never forget that moment when I became a Born Again Christian. This had been the pinnacle in my journey—an overflowing experience like that during my visit to the Church of St. Photini, which I described earlier, where I heard God promise me, "Your life will be filled to overflowing!" And then, another one happened a couple of years ago, after my monastery experience. A woman extended an invitation to me on a dating website, "Ever had a blind date? Try me!"

THE BLIND HELPS THE LOST TO SEE

It has been a gift to learn what is important in life and to understand that these are the things you cannot see! God changed everything in my life through the eyes of a blind woman of God.

My amazing wife

Several things transpired to help me change my vision of myself and give me the ability to overcome my fears. This faith changed me from being focused on myself to be able to love again. It took me from living in a monastery for almost two years to marrying a devout Christian woman.

My wife, Cherise, who has been blind from birth, helps me to see the world in a whole new way, and she opens vistas of imagination and creativity that I had only dreamed were possible. The example she embodies shows me every day that I can live fully in the moment with a single-minded focus, without the distractions of this world.

Since the two of us are unable to see things together, she can experience me by touching me, and she even knows when I look directly into her eyes. One time she told me the look I was giving her was penetrating to the very depths of her heart! Our conversations together flow endlessly because my ability to communicate has always been strong, but not like hers. She is a master communicator. In fact, she is one of the best I have ever met. Verbal expression is one of her greatest strengths.

One day I fell asleep in her arms and was basking in her love when I woke up to hear her praying to God. She didn't know I was awake, and in a whisper, she was quietly thanking God for bringing me into her life. What a gift it was to hear, and I never told her that I heard her until I wrote this.

I feel profound thankfulness to God who has blessed my life story with a loving relationship. I adore this woman, and I have found a deep perception and experience open up to me by God Almighty. Sometimes the blind help the lost to see. God changed everything for me through the deep perceptions of this blind woman. She has taught me so much about God's presence in our lives.

It is fascinating to understand that my wife teaches about not walking in spiritual blindness. From the very start, I believe God promised me when I first met her that He would show me a world I had never seen before through her eyes. She is teaching me to see *His* world around me more clearly than ever before. It's the invisible things in life that make us truly appreciate God's presence in our lives.

Ma Cherie, which means "my sweetheart," calls herself a daredevil, and what a great adventure this has been with her. Action and adventure are now my new reality—not the taking in of empty visual stimuli. It has been a gift to learn what is important in life, and those are the things that I can't see. I should have known that zip-lining on our honeymoon or jet-skiing on the ocean would be our new normal. Love is an incredible reality when you experience it from someone who sees it from a spiritual perspective.

Without her being able to see it, we can experience it together. What is truly amazing is our relationship is focused on experiencing life together, taking in all of life joined together as one. We impart our different perspectives of living life to be filled to overflowing as one.

As I said, the conversations between us flow endlessly. I am reminded of how this is likened to my relationship with my Heavenly Father, whom I cannot see. See our pictures on Facebook: #CheriseandPaul.

This quote by Henry David Thoreau has given me great inspiration: "Could a greater miracle

My lovely wife on the beach in Mexico

take place than for us to look through each other's eyes for an instant?"

Are you at an intense time in your life? I pray for all those who are isolated and who desire love in their lives. Maybe it is time to reach out to the unseen but all-knowing God, whom I know as our Lord and Savior Jesus Christ. He desires to live in everyones' heart like the love that lives in a newfound relationship. It's a young love that can be lived day by day, never stagnating or dying but living throughout eternity because I know He cares for you because He cares for me.

So much happened after I met Cherise and we started dating. That was really an interesting time. We were dealing not only with the fears of the pandemic but with messaging that we sensed was more rhetoric and seemed like propaganda. Cherise and I still wanted to go forward with our event, and we were introduced at the wedding reception as "The COVID-Defiant Couple." In regard to the wedding ceremony, a lot of churches were not even meeting in June of 2020. Minneapolis, just seventy miles away, had seen riots seventeen days before. The church we chose to be married in was small enough that it would comfortably seat thirty-five to forty people. We set up three tents outside, and people could stay there or go downstairs to the fellowship hall, or upstairs to the sanctuary. We also streamed our wedding since it was during the plandemic. *Yes, PLANDEMIC.*

Our wedding reception send-off

We live-streamed the event through a new Facebook group I had created for the church. It was amazing to see how a Facebook group can make a message go from an average of thirty to forty close friends to more than four hundred people. They could see it whenever they wanted to. We decided to not do a reception line after the service and instead set up our photographers and a videographer to film and record our interactions with those who felt comfortable with us in a close setting. We were praying that no one would come down with the virus, and thankfully our prayers that day were heard. Praise be to God!

There were people tuning in online from all over the country and even internationally. Quite a few of my high school classmates and some mission directors in Africa whom I helped also tuned into the service. The convenience is nice. However, the lack of connectedness falls short. Is there something that has been destroyed by all of our online captivation? I'm grateful for the opportunity to connect with so many people online, and I'm glad that my technological gifts have helped me throughout my career and ministry to give back when God has so generously given to me and my family.

Me with one of my four grandsons

Most people are not even close to "killing it" on any form of digital media because it appears very complicated and much too challenging for them to be successful. There are way too many choices and offers that are nothing more than empty promises. In my experience, I find the greatest failure is for people to think they know what they are doing when they really don't. Many people want to learn our techniques, and we are more than willing to share our secrets with our members. Discover the possibilities you may be missing out on by contacting us at KillingItOnline.com.

CONCLUSION

ONE OF THE most formative experiences of my life was a rock-climbing adventure I took when I was twenty-three years old. Located in the Gallatin Mountain Range of Western Montana, the trek involved a group of about fifteen students and young adults who were embarking on a life-changing experience.

Our instructor facilitated learning, not by trusting in our intellect but rather by believing in our hearts what we sensed was inspiration from within. For instance, you may face a tough climb where the rocks appear perilous. You can approach the challenge from a sense-knowledge perspective and try to analyze your way up the rock, or you can do it another way. Our instructor's approach was quite unique because he believed that you can "climb by inspiration."

Our instructor's famous five words were, "Just believe God and GO!"

As we were instructed in this approach, we grew very close as a team. Our climbing coach empowered us to believe in these powerful principles, as our lives depended upon them. We learned a different way to climb the rocks, using neither techniques nor style but by in-spirit action. As we trusted in our inspiration, even more of it began to flow as it increased in momentum.

We did not evaluate the climb as one would see a rock, analyze it, and try to logically figure it out. We did not focus on our physical strength or mental ability to get up the rock. A verse from Proverbs became so completely real for me:

> *Trust in the Lord with all your heart, and*
> *lean not on your own understanding; in*
> *all your ways acknowledge Him, And He*
> *shall direct your paths.*
> —Proverbs 3:5 (KJV)[29]

I did not forget what I had learned by the end of the week. Instead, I have carried it with me throughout my

---

[29] https://www.kingjamesbibleonline.org/Proverbs-3-5/

life. Being a young man who loved Christ and wanting to serve Him, this was without a doubt the most unforgettable spiritual learning experience I would ever have.

We were encouraged to listen to the "small still voice" as we moved up "The Rock." What we desired to know at the time was given to us, when we trusted Him. Could this be the fulfillment I had been looking for? Was I being personally taught by the Holy Spirit and my Lord Jesus Christ? We found as we practiced the principles of trusting that the inspiration was not outside of ourselves but within.

Toward the end of the week, some experienced climbers joined us for a rather tough climb. After they watched us climb for some time, they asked us a telling question: "How many years have you all been climbing?"

We said that we had only been climbing for a couple days.

They immediately refuted it: "No way!"

That's when the principle of believing in God, relying on His inspiration, and trusting in His gentle leading revealed our newfound instincts, which led us to greater heights.

I have found a wide plethora of opportunities for learning today. Personally, I gravitate to a type of learning that I call inspirational learning. However, I can tell you that the setbacks have taught me more about life than the successes. Needless to say, from that day forward, inspiration has been a way of life for me.

Ideas in marketing these days are a dime a dozen, but a creative and innovative campaign can transform your marketing message into an enormous windfall. What would a $10,000 idea do for your business if it produced $100,000 or, better yet, $1,000,000?

Coming up with ideas for your business is what we do best. Sign up for a strategy session and see what can happen to transform your business and your life. Go to our booking website: NeuStreams.com

CREATING A LASTING LEGACY

This bears repeating: When I was in training in gymnastics for the Olympics, there were many things I learned from my high school coach Jack Harris and university coach Francis Allen. However, the impact my own life made on others is what I completely did not realize until recently.

I learned this when I was told it by a man I mentored over forty years ago. Mark Walter, who was a freshman in high school when I was a senior, proceeded at dinner to tell me how he broke all my state championship records in gymnastics. We hadn't seen each other in all those years.

Mark said to me, "Paul, you changed my life!" He told me that he had learned from the principles I practiced back then. He said I truly changed all aspects of his life. When Mark shared this realization with me, I discovered the true meaning in life: helping each other to ascend to a new level in life is what it is all about!

My daughter (left), me (center), and my son (back right)

My prayer and belief is that what I share can resonate within you, and that it can truly inspire you. Through your action and desire, coupled with believing, a dynamic change in your life will cause you to grow and become the person you have dreamed of.

Now I can offer business owners a lot more with Google than I did back when I sold yellow pages. I have seen there is a lot of power in "KILLING IT ONLINE" with search engine marketing. You can take advantage of where the lion's share of traffic is, and that is definitely with Google, Facebook, and Instagram. It is a tremendous business opportunity for young millennials but also great for retired people.

Learn more about becoming one of our Certified Search Pros. I believe it is the greatest part-time opportunity in the world! My pursuit of the online industry produced the parent company of NeuStream Media, which features Killing It Online, the platform for all of our different business ventures.

7 STEPS FOR OVERFLOWING SUCCESS— MY MOST POWERFUL SECRET TO LIFE'S MEANING AND FULFILLMENT

You can fly like an eagle to heights unknown!
Photo used with permission: Craig Goodwin

My main motivation for this book was to help those who have gone through an incredible loss learn how to recover. Although going from lost to found is just the beginning, it is a giant step toward getting back on track with your life. Much like some of the business owners I have counseled, you have to make some bold moves with confidence by moving from a state of inaction to one of action, which activates the miraculous.

Go beyond the imagination and take action, so you can overflow with an incredible amount of momentum and fulfillment!

1. MAKE A DECISION!

Because you need a desire and purpose to do something, making a decision is the first key to momentum. What is something that you have always wanted, deep down?

Can you see yourself doing something extraordinary? Most people don't, or can't, as they don't want to create waves, stand out, or be noticed. They want to be normal. Rising up or ascending takes a quality of fearlessness.

Thankfulness is a key ingredient for receiving any type of inspiration or inner motivation. This will start the process of momentum.

2. TAKE ACTION—GET MOVING!

Second, what separates the achiever from the non-achiever is focus and taking action. Unfortunately, the type of motivation that generates fast action is often not beneficial.

You also need to be sure that your motivation is a desire to accomplish something significant, rather than an ulterior motive—for instance, only wanting to drive up sales without putting the customer first.

3. BE FEARLESS & COURAGEOUS!

The one thing that stops people the most is fear! However, all great and successful people have one common core element: they have learned how to control their fears.

Many times, this is nothing more than controlling your thoughts. However, this takes a formadable amount of self-discipline!

4. RELY ON YOUR INSPIRATION

Our inspiration is a very personal thing to us. It is amazing to see people's reactions when you ask them the question, "What inspires you?" For instance, one person told me, "My five-year-old son; he inspires me!" As it was in her case, our inspiration often comes from a love we have for someone or something besides ourselves.

Our most dependable inspirations for giving and receiving are based upon pure intentions. Belongingness in our relationships is our greatest motivation!

5. DEVELOP YOUR ENTHUSIASM

Besides inspiration, I have found that enthusiasm, which I think of as *en-Theo*, is crucial. I got my inspiration from this quote from Earl Nightingale: "The word 'enthusiasm' comes from the Greek word 'entheos,' which means the God within. And the happiest, most interesting people are those who have found the secret of maintaining their enthusiasm, that God within."[30] *Theo* is the Greek word for God, and *en* means within. *En-Theo* means "God energized within!" Since I was seventeen, my desire has been to not just be filled with the Holy Spirit but to be "filled to overflowing" in all aspects of my life.

When Christ spoke to Photini, the woman of Samaria at the well, she was not just filled with "living water," she was filled to overflowing.

> *Jesus answered and said to her,*
> *"Whoever drinks of this water will thirst*
> *again, but whoever drinks of the water*
> *that I shall give him will never thirst.*
> *But the water that I shall give him will*
> *become in him a fountain of water*
> *springing up into everlasting life."*
> —John 4:13—14

---

[30] https://www.optimize.me/quotes/earl-nightingale/the-word-enthusiasm-comes-from-the-greek-word-entheos-which

6. BUILD EACH OTHER UP

One summer after high school, I worked at an Exide battery factory. On the tour for new employees, I learned about how the large batteries were made—several smaller ones were linked together, which created a multiplication of power. When you link two 300-amp batteries, you don't have 600 amps of power; you have 900 amps.

The same thing happens when you team up with someone to build enthusiasm and raise your collective momentum. Teaming up with your Heavenly Father is the most powerful combination, especially when you do it on a daily basis. If you are married and joined in Christ, then you can grow and develop into a three-way powerhouse.

7. MASTERING YOUR MIND

In classical Greek literature, the mind is equated to a dog being let loose during a game. This dog—your mind—needs control, which requires a mental collar with a short leash. In some cases, setting boundaries is not a popular idea. However, limiting negative thoughts and speaking what you desire will truly define and shape your future self.

THE WELL OF OUR LIFE

We fill our wells with what is most important to us, the treasures we give the highest value to. These material things bring us what we believe to be the greatest satisfaction, but they fall short. My wife was saying the invisible things in life are the things that last: God's love,

Jacob's Well, in Palestine

hope, and faith. She can't see the sky, but she can feel the wind in her hair. You can have sounds, music, all kinds of things that you can fill your life with, that satisfy you.

You can be a big fan of a football, hockey, or basketball team. You can follow celebrity, you can follow fame, and you can even become a bodybuilder. You can put all your faith in following some religion, but I have found that what really gives us the best, most genuine satisfaction, is simply our connectedness.

And so, this is when we are connected to something or someone, a group of people or a family, that's something you are a part of, that you contribute to and help grow.

Wells can have holes in them and all kinds of leaks; worst of all, they can be contaminated. But nothing satisfies a soul like Jesus Christ.

> *For My people have committed two evils:*
> *They have forsaken Me, the fountain*
> *of living waters, And hewn themselves*
> *cisterns—broken cisterns that*
> *can hold no water.*
> —Jeremiah 2:13 (NKJV)[31]

It is scary when you are not sure if what you are drinking is safe or not. If you have arsenic in your well, it can be toxic to the point of your demise, even in a short amount of time. Some impurities take time to destroy our health, and we may not even know it is happening. The way to clean a well is to introduce pure and good water into it in overflowing abundance.

Sometimes our wells get filled up with other things. In the Old Testament, Abraham and Isaac had enemies who would come and fill their wells with dirt. Then Abraham and Isaac had to re-dig them. Sometimes we have to do that in our own lives. We have to clear out the rubble and the things that are

---

[31] https://biblia.com/bible/nkjv/jeremiah/2/13

keeping us from getting our life-source from the well. It all comes down to this, just like the Scriptures say!

"Believe in me so that rivers of living water will burst out from within you, flowing from your innermost being..."
—John 7:38 (TPT)[32]

The things that really give meaning to life are the personal things, such as relationships and being connected. When we exclude God from our lives, we are going to end up empty and lost. When we fill our lives with the invisible things of God, He will fill us with the overflowing of our souls. My encouragement to you is this: Look for something good to come out of the negatives in life!

It is amazing how I met and got to be good friends with Paul and Cherise. We met at my nail salon in spring of 2020. Even though we didn't know each other very long it was meaningful to me because we have similar interests and we love America and we love to do things for the community and society, which is my happiness. I do things knowing

---

[32] https://www.bible.com/bible/1849/JHN.7.38.TPT

it will build a better life for all of the things that come from my heart. Unexpectedly, after meeting Paul and Cherise I have received so much love and help from them. After only a few times of meeting with them, they helped me build a website and gave me good ideas to help my business of U.S. Nails and get more customers. Even though they are busy with their work, they have always had time for me.

I would like to very much express my sincere thanks to my good friends Paul and Cherise, who have turned into my dear customers. It is the greetings and smiles that have warmed my heart. It means a lot to me when they ask how I am doing or how the salon is doing. Because of their help, they are a gift from above to help me overcome difficulties and struggles in my life. I will always cherish their friendship! Thank you for always being there when I need help. A thank you will probably never be enough for all the help you guys have given me, but I will keep you all in my heart forever!
—Selena (U.S. Nails and Nail Salon)

FINAL THOUGHTS

Congratulations on reaching the end of this book! Through the stories and experiences I have recounted, you can now understand the life skills needed to be a successful business owner and entrepreneur.

For me, this book has been mainly about the inspiration of God in my life. It also has been about my personal ups and downs of going from lost to found and then filled to overflowing. Following His lead, acting on His inspiration, and seeing the abundant fruit harvested from His ideas has made me a believer in one thing:

But God has chosen the foolish things of the world to put to shame the wise, and God has chosen the weak things of the world to put to shame the things which are mighty; and the base things of the world and the things which are despised God has chosen, and the things which are not, to bring to nothing the things that are, that no flesh should glory in His presence. But of Him you are in Christ Jesus, who became

*for us wisdom from God—and righteous-
ness and sanctification and redemption—*
—1 Corinthians 1:27–30 (KJV)[33]

I do not claim His ideas as mine. I have come to know this inspiration in His ever so small, still voice, and I know beyond a shadow of a doubt that He cares for you. I believe the Lord desires to converse with you because He loves you with an everlasting love and wants to fill you to overflowing! Now the only thing to do is—ask! The simplest prayer I ever heard someone pray was the greatest. It was simply this: "Lord, please be with me."

Ultimately, whether you are adapting to a changing industry or finding a way to express yourself and your ideas, what you have to remember is to claim victory from fear.

You may find that you are being held back by fear—and will even miss opportunities when they present themselves. You realize that this is a mental as well as spiritual battle that can be overcome. Mistakes can be learning opportunities; they do not spell the end of your career.

---

[33] https://biblia.com/bible/nkjv/1-corinthians/1/27–30

Although Willy Loman in *Death of a Salesman* did not respond well to change, you are equipped to take a different, better path. Balancing a confident personality with a respectful, listening attitude requires a lot of bravery, but it is the one trait that will make you stand out. Whether you adapt to the change or even find an opportunity through it, you can believe and keep pressing forward.

Once you reach this point, you can develop momentum to succeed in both your business and personal life. One way to do this is through sound thoughts with well-worded messaging. This requires focused communication and the ability to actively listen. Remember, meekness is not weakness, and we all should continue to be coachable, every day.

When I worked through the three principles presented in *Death of a Yellow Page Salesman*, which are (1) going from lost to found, (2) developing momentum, and (3) overflowing in your business and your life, it wasn't a smooth ride for me, as shown by my stories. I often struggled with self-doubt and had to continuously adapt to changes in my industry, especially during the shift from the yellow pages in print to everything being online.

However, through gentle inspiration from God, and a hope to help others, I was able to overcome these struggles. As I realized that my abilities in marketing were making a positive impact on the world, I continued to stay motivated. This is something I believe anyone who is willing to try can do. Whether you are helping small businesses with their sales or promoting a beneficial product or service through your own business, you will help others on their own paths to success. Through the practical advice I have provided and common pitfalls I have pointed out, you are now well equipped for success.

My wife and I enjoy speaking, coaching, and conducting workshops and seminars. We aspire to support and teach business owners, entrepreneurs, and professionals throughout the world. Click here for our contact information and for booking: PaulNeustrom.com

DEDICATION AND ACKNOWLEDGMENTS

I want to thank Ashley Kammermeier, my editor, and Elianna Wood for content editing. Abby Sherman for her photography expertise. I also want to thank a very special person for his

help for author coaching and being my Book Creation Manager, Matthew Schnarr. Thanks also go to Steve Fata, the Creative and Technical Director, and the entire team at Best Seller Publishing, including CEO Rob Kosberg, for your patience and encouragement. My gratitude is immeasurable for my personal mentor and business inspiration, Kim Walsh Phillips of Powerful Professionals. Finally, many thanks to my two spiritual leaders, Dave Hauer and Evangelist

Dean Goossen of Awakening Hope Ministries. Your guidance and inspiration have been pivotal in my turnaround, and I thank God for both of your lives.

This book is dedicated to those readers who are not where they want to be in life—not in reference to your location but rather to your own fulfillment. It is written for those who desire more from life and are open to discovering their true calling and purpose. It is for those individuals, business owners, entrepreneurs—those who are looking for more growth in their lives. It is designed for those desiring help, who are not afraid to ask, and are willing to try. This is written for entrepreneurs and business owners who exude originality and personality. You are life's breath of fresh air.

This book is for all those who have gone through a loss and desire a miraculous change in their personal lives and their businesses, which I see as inextricably intertwined.

Most importantly, this is committed and given in thanksgiving to my Lord and Savior Jesus Christ.

To my children, grandchildren, and to my departed parents and grandparents.

Thank you to all who have offered their inspiration, support, patience, and encouragement. Most importantly, to Cherise, my soul mate—with undying love, I dedicate this to you! This book undoubtedly would have never been published without encouragement and gentle guidance from you. I love the story of us. You reached out your hand to me, and we began our journey together. Along the way, I discovered that wherever God takes us, the shelter of you will always be my home. You are my storybook love, the woman of my dreams. Our life together is my happily-ever-after.[34] Sweetheart, I love you!

The word *ström* means "stream" or "river" in Swedish, so a name like Nordstrom would mean "north stream" or "north river." On Ellis Island my ancestors had their name changed from Nystrom to Neustrom, and "ny" or "neu" means "new." It meant

---

[34] https://www.hallmark.com/cards/greeting-cards/i-love-the-story-of-us-birth-day-card-for-her-459FBD4233.html

a new start to a river of adventure as they started a whole new life in America.

We are only taking a few business clients who are looking to grow.

To contact us for speaking engagements and seminars on unplugging and tapping into the creative energies of God Almighty, look us up: PaulNeustrom.com

Paul T. Neustrom—known as the
Never Say Die Guy